LANDMARK COLLECTOR'S

Lost House
North Staffordshire

Cathryn Walton & Lindsey Porter

Opposite: Highfield Hall

LANDMARK COLLECTOR'S LIBRARY

Lost Houses of North Staffordshire

Cathryn Walton & Lindsey Porter

Landmark Publishing

Published by

Ashbourne Hall, Cokayne Ave
Ashbourne, Derbyshire, DE6 1EJ England
Tel: (01335) 347349 Fax: (01335) 347303
e-mail: landmark@clara.net
web site: www.landmarkpublishing.co.uk

13 ISBN: 978-1-84306-195-3
10 ISBN: 1-84306-195-3

British Library Cataloguing in Publication Data: a catalogue record for this book is available from the British Library.

Print: Gutenburg Press, Malta

Design & reproduction by: James Allsopp

Front cover: Knypersley Hall, c. 1840 (Wm Salt Library).

Back cover: Dilhorne Hall.

Page 1: Alton Abbey c. 1820.

Page 3: Entrance front, Highfield Hall, Leek.

Acknowledgements

The authors wish to thank all those who have assisted with the research for this book. In particular the following: T. Alexander (Belmont); Apedale Mining Museum; Ash Hall Nursing and Residential Care Home; Mr M Brooks (Lightoaks); Alban Burton (Paynsley); Cheadle Library staff; Faith Cleverdon; Mrs Hilary Corby (Shaw); Mr and Mrs Featherstone (Yoxall Lodge); Father Michael Fisher (Alton Castle, Alton Towers); Hon. J. Greenall (Wootton); Horton Lodge Special School; Robin and Charles Hurt (Throwley); Leek Library staff; Mrs Mary Minshall (Paynsley); National Monuments Record; William Podmore (Consall); George Short (Cheadle area houses); Margaret and Edgar Smith (Ilam); Stoke-on-Trent Central Library, Hanley; Peter Trewhitt (Wootton Gates); William Salt Library, Stafford; John Walker (Crakemarsh); Keith Warburton (Highfield); Derek Wheelhouse; Peter Wilson (Oakamoor area houses and Cotton); John Woodward (Paynsley).

Contents

INTRODUCTION

For a long time, Lindsey Porter had been collecting photographs and wanted to know more about many country houses, which had been demolished in the Staffordshire Moorlands. Cathryn Walton had been doing something similar on houses in Leek and it seemed the logical thing to combine resources and further our research. This seemed all the more appropriate following the success of our four recent books (1).

Neither of us has an architectural background, although Lindsey qualified as a Chartered Surveyor. This book allows us to show some of the fine properties that have been lost (either demolished or no longer used as a dwelling) through the illustrations we have been able to bring together. We have added text to some to give a little of the history of the house. We hope that this will encourage others to investigate, to unearth more on the buildings, their construction and the people who lived in them. A second section brings together photographs of other houses – a limited number only. Most, but not all, of the houses selected were country seats, but a selection of urban properties are also included. The southern boundary we have adopted and the inclusion of some urban properties as well as country seats is entirely arbitrary. More Leek houses have been included in Cath's *Spirit of Leek: Volume 4*.

Between 1870 and 1990, it has been estimated that some 2,000 country seats have been lost countrywide and it was surely higher than this. (2) Of the 74 houses included here, 33 have been demolished, substantially reduced or are in ruins and that excludes properties removed to make way for a new house. The nadir may well have been 1934–35, when at least Apedale, Ilam and Wootton Halls, Calwich Abbey and Yoxall Lodge were lost in North Staffordshire alone. The latest seems to have been Crakemarsh Hall which was eventually lost in a fire. A new age has seen the refurbishment of many country houses and the rebuilding of one – Wootton Hall. This has been rebuilt in traditional style and in stone, although to a different design, the work being completed in 2002.

It has been pleasing to find a painting of the rear of Beresford Hall and a photograph of Throwley Hall, probably dated 1858, which reduces the time-frame in which the majority of this house was demolished. The discovery of many photographs taken of the interior of Rolleston Hall has allowed a comparison with those of Ilam. Interior views are not common and this is regrettable, both from the point of view of style, but also of changes in fashion.

Nonetheless, we hope that this eclectic collection contains some surprises and provides a measure of enjoyment. Any curiosity or criticism about the omission of particular houses, eg Barlaston, we have to take on the chin. We have not set out to cover every large house in the area and our selection has been subjective. It should be noted that this is essentially a book of photographs and no attempt has been made to give complete histories of houses. Nearly all the properties shown herein, where they survive, are not open to the public and privacy should be respected at all times.

Although reproduction rights do not come cheap, we have tried to introduce some illustrations of pre-photography days. The William Salt Library at Stafford has a collection of paintings and drawings of immense value to historians. The National Monuments Record of English Heritage has millions (literally) of photographic images, many still uncatalogued. It particularly houses the National Buildings Survey Collection of photographs and those of *Country Life*. Its 'Red Box' Collection records photographs of buildings on a parish basis and is open for researchers.

• The William Salt Library, Eastgate St, Stafford, ST16 2LZ. Situated adjacent to the Staffordshire Record Office. Images from this collection used are are on pages: 23(T & B), 35(B), 37, 44, 59(B), 66(T), 67, 68, 77(T), 98 & 99.
• English Heritage National Monuments Record, Kemble Drive, Gt Western Village, Swindon, Wiltshire, SN2 2GZ. Images from this collection used are on pages: 54, 122-124 (all).

Cathryn Walton & Lindsey Porter

Part 1: The Houses

Albion House, Old Hall Street, Hanley

Demolished

Situated near the former Town Hall (previously the Queen's Hotel). A late-Georgian house (?1830s) of a rather plain design, it had an attractive set of iron gates, with a boundary wall surmounted by an iron palisade fronting the street pavement. It was located in Old Hall Street, at that time a part of Shelton.

On 20th August 1842, the house was destroyed by Chartist rioters. It was attacked and set on fire, with no attempt made to save the property; even the fire engine "was not fetched." Josiah Wedgwood, upon hearing of the altercation, dispatched his pottery fire engine, but the mob prevented its progress. The house was reduced to a roofless shell.

All the furniture, valuable paintings and books worth several thousand pounds were lost, according to the *Staffordshire Advertiser*. It was the home of William Parker, a local magistrate, who unfortunately became the focus of the attack. The *Staffordshire Advertiser* reported that the mob destroyed several large houses in the area, burning and looting the contents. Needless to say, the following October, fellow magistrates meted out retribution at Stafford Assizes. George Wilcox was transported for 21 years; Adam Wood and Edward Ellis were transported for 10 years. Elijah Simpson and Thomas Turner also received 21 years transportation and John Silito went down for 12 months. More were charged with other offences (see under Apedale Hall).

Right: Albion House being destroyed by the mob

Alton Castle, Alton

Castle mostly demolished/Rebuilt and now a school

Paradoxically, mention Alton Castle and people think of the Pugin-built building of the 1840s. Compared to a Rhineland castle, it is certainly dramatic in its situation, although external maintenance must be a nightmare. However, this is not the Castle from which the current building takes its name. For several centuries, this was the site of a Norman castle occupied as a fortified house by the de Verduns and their descendants. It was built c. 1175 by Bertram de Verdun, who also founded Croxden Abbey to the south.

Its demise resulted from its being garrisoned for the king during the Civil War, when it was held by some 50 soldiers. However, by February 1645 it was in the hands of the Parliament, with Mr Thomas Salt the Governor of the castle. The castle subsequently fell into disrepair as seen on the drawing by Buck (see p11).

The ruin was further reduced by John, the 16th Earl of Shrewsbury prior to the construction of the current building. The latter was built within the castle wall of which remnants remain, including almost the full height of the external side of one of the western towers (illustrated opposite). The presence of the remains of this Norman castle will perhaps come as a surprise to many readers.

The current building is a Roman Catholic school but had been built at least in part as a house. Alton Castle was previously known by the earlier name of the village of Alton – Alveton.

Work on the new castle began in 1847, (1) quite possibly for the Earl's nephew and heir, Bertram or his wife if he pre-deceased her. (See also, Cotton Hall, p58). At the time of the Alton Towers Estate dispersal sale, 1919, the Castle was let to the Misses MacDonnel and Verdon on a lease for 21 years from 29th September 1903. The sisters were running the forerunner of the current Roman Catholic School. (2)

It is possible that Bertram did not live here, for the Earl may have died before it was completed. It was some time before Bertram was able to claim the estate owing to the will being contested and when he finally took possession on 25th February 1860 he had Alton Towers at his disposal.

left: Remains of steps in the outer wall of the castle, west side

Original tower and curtain wall of the Norman castle

The south side of the remaining tower

Above: The ruined original castle drawn by S & N Buck in 1731

Below: Taken from adjacent to the lodge to Alton Towers. The castle is seen with its east front dramatically sited above the Churnet Valley. The south tower was never finished. This view is c. 100 years ago

The east front

The chapel of the Victorian rebuild of the castle (right). Original castle curtain wall to the left

Alton Towers, Alton

Ruin

Three houses have stood on the site of the Alton Towers Amusement Park. The great pile known as Alton Towers was the third house, but incredibly it incorporated much of its two predecessors. A full and impressive account of all three houses has been written by Michael Fisher (1), which is recommended. Michael is a leading authority on the Gothic Revival movement, both secular and ecclesiastical. (See p.158 for details of his new book on the latter in Staffordshire). It was in this county that the movement developed ecclesiastically, five leading architects producing their best work here. However, the movement was not so well represented in housing – although Alton Towers (incorporating Alton Abbey), the nearby Alton Castle, Butterton Hall, Snelston Hall (just in Derbyshire) and Ilam Hall are examples.

Fortunately, Alveton Lodge, the first house on the Alton Towers site, features on Buck's drawing of Alton Castle of 1731. Michael Fisher notes that the surviving elements of this building – the east wall and circular tower – portray early 18th century architecture, but also notes that Plot refers to the house in 1686 (2), so it may have been altered prior to the 1830s. The circular tower is visible on the 1731 drawing. There were two parts to the Lodge – the formal part, used occasionally by the Talbots and another used by their steward (estate manager).

The development of Alton Abbey began in 1811 (by the Earl of Shrewsbury) and took ten years to complete. Already much development work in the garden had taken place. Comparison of the north front of Alton Abbey and the later Towers shows how the former was integrated into the latter, a major change being the conversion of the Abbey's entrance hall into the dining room by Pugin in the 1840s. Pugin arrived late on the scene (in 1837) during the construction of the Towers, which began in the early 1830s.

In the late 19th century, the house had passed to the Chetwyn-Talbots, whose main house was Ingestre Hall, not the massive house at Alton Towers, which must have been far too large for domestic comfort. A late 19th century vogue was using large houses as amusement parks (see Clough Hall) and Alton Towers was used similarly. Much of the huge estate was sold in 1918 and the rest, including the Towers, went in 1924. Used as an amusement park prior to World War II, the Towers was requisitioned by the Army between 1939 and 1951. A year after this all the timber and metal was ripped out (except for the Chapel and dining room roofs) thereby destroying a priceless national asset. Today, the walls have been stabilised and the architectural features remaining in the Chapel and dining room have been restored. The house now sits in the middle of the popular theme park. It is an iconic reminder of an earlier, more formal age in the middle of 21st century commercialism and conspicuous recreational consumption.

Left: An early view of Alveton Lodge, the original house, from S & N Buck's drawing of Alton Castle, 1731. This building still survives within the main structure of Alton Towers

Above: Alton Abbey c. 1820. Drawn originally by Thomas Allason, this lithograph was by Hopwood. (Alton Towers Archive)

Below: Alton Towers. Comparison with the above illustration shows the areas of redevelopment in the 1830s

The great window of the dining room on the north-east front

Above: The house from the east, on the drive to the stables

Below: The north-east front from the lake

Above: The Loggia Arcade (left) and Le Refuge (right), with the Garden Conservatory above. The Nine Muses and other statues adorn the balustrade above. A few of the 179 stone or iron vases included in the dispersal sale may be seen here. The columns of Le Refuge came from the entrance to Alveton Lodge

Left: Looking from the head of the garden towards the house. The round tower in the middle of the roofline is part of Alveton Lodge

Above: The garden and house with the Swiss Cottage to the left. The last photograph was taken from top left, just above the Garden Conservatory. The Canal Pond is in the middle of the photograph

Below: A lovely view towards the Pagoda Fountain

Apedale Hall, off Loomer Road, Chesterton
Demolished

In 1825 Richard Edensor Heathcote, who lived at Longton Hall, began to build a new home on an elevated site in Apedale looking out over the Cheshire plain. This house, finished in 1826, was of a fairly basic style due to financial constraints. By planting trees and small coppices he created parkland and by 1834, he had improved the outlook from the hall by filling in four old coal pits and removing spoil. (1) The hall was built on or near to the site of an earlier building as its foundations (at least in part) were found during the construction.

Richard E. Heathcote was the grandson of Michael Heathcote of Buxton and Hartington; who had married Rachel Edensor of Hartington. Their son, Sir John Edensor Heathcote, who lived at Longton Hall, married Ann Gresley. It was John's son Richard who built Apedale Hall. He also married a Gresley, Emma Sophia who died in 1813. His second wife was Lady Elizabeth Keith Lindsay, daughter of the 6th Earl of Balcarres and the 23rd Earl of Crawford, whom he married in 1815.

In 1841 Richard Heathcote and his third wife Susan were at Apedale on the night of the census, together with 6 male and 10 female servants.

On 20th July 1842 Chartist rioters surrounded the hall after they had been to the Apedale mine and closed down the workings. Forty of Heathcote's servants together with farmhands and workmen held the mob at bay, protecting the terrified family and servants inside the hall. The mob dispersed after Richard Heathcote and his agent arrived, followed by a detachment of the 3rd Dragoons and 60th Regiment of Rifles. In early October 1842, some 274 men went on trial at Stafford Assizes for their part in the disorders in the Potteries. Of these 60 men were acquitted, 154 sent to jail for varying sentences and 54 were transported. Eleven of these were transported for life. (2) Richard enlarged the hall, adding a library and a banqueting hall. In the windows of the banqueting hall he had placed four stained glass heraldic designs. The four shields depicted: 1) Lindsay: his second wife's family and mother of Elizabeth; 2) Edensor Heathcote; 3) Bowyer-Gresley; from whom he was descended and 4) Heathcote-Sandford; in honour of his eldest son's marriage in 1837. The hall was finally completed in 1845.

Richard died in 1850 leaving the hall to his son, John Edensor Heathcote, who occupied the hall in 1851. (3)

The 1860 Kelly's *Post Office Directory* describes Apedale Hall, the seat of John Edensor Heathcote, as "a handsome modern mansion of Tudor, Norman and Elizabethan styles of architecture, on an eminence commanding beautiful and extensive views". John Heathcote and his wife, Mary Ann, employed a butler and nine other servants at Apedale in 1861. By 1870 John's nephew, Justinian Heathcote-Edwards, was living at Apedale. He changed his surname to Edwards Heathcote in 1870 to satisfy the terms of his uncle's will. In 1881 four Heathcote children, aged from nine to four years old, were in residence with servants including a butler, housekeeper and a nurse. Justinian left Apedale Hall in 1892 but returned in 1899. Captain Justinian Edwards Heathcote, MP for North Staffordshire, died in 1928.

John Spencer Edwards-Heathcote, Justinian's son, married Valentina Alida Frazer in 1911. They spent part of their honeymoon at Apedale Hall, making them the last Heathcotes to live there. (4)

From 1928 Mr Hill, the manager of the Midland Coal, Coke and Iron Company, rented the hall but in 1933 the hall and estate were put up for sale. The hall had four principal rooms plus a banqueting hall, nine bedrooms and seventeen servants' rooms. A buyer for the hall could not be found and it gradually deteriorated before being demolished in 1934. An article on heraldic glass in Apedale (5) states that "the Apedale Hall is in the process of disruption and the hall itself is in decay, and if it is not pulled down it will soon fall in ruins". The demolition sale of the hall took place on 23rd October 1934, when the heraldic glass panels relating to the Heathcote family were sold for less than £10. (6)

Above: The house before it was remodelled in 1845

Below: The final form of the house

Aqualate Hall, Forton, near Newport

Rebuilt, now reduced

An earlier hall stood on a low hill overlooking Aqualate Mere. Sir Thomas Skrymsher rebuilt this first hall in c. 1600. When he died, in 1633 the hall passed by marriage to the Baldwyns. The old house had three storeys, and a north front with small gables to the parapet. Two semi-octagonal bays finished with balustrades flanked the principal doorway (see below). The Baldwyns built the stable court in the 18th century. They sold the hall to the trustees of John Fletcher in 1791. The house was partly remodelled in 1800 and 1805, when the north bays were removed, sash windows inserted and two flanking wings added, while John Fenton Fletcher was still a minor. Later he changed his surname to Fenton-Boughey. (1) When he came of age he commissioned John Nash to carry out a large addition to the west making the hall three times its original size. Nash remodelled the house in an extravagant Gothic style with pinnacled buttresses, stucco and window tracery. The new extension had polygonal turrets with castellated parapets and ogee domes. Thomas Fletcher Fenton Boughey, John's son, lived here until his death in 1880. In 1841 he employed twenty nine servants at Aqualate. Thomas died without issue and his brothers Reverend George Boughey and Sir William Fletcher Boughey occupied the hall in 1908 and 1912 respectively. (2) A fire destroyed the west extension, designed by Nash, in 1910 together with part of the original 17th century building. In the late 1920s the house was restored in a simplified Jacobean style. The top storey was removed and all traces of Nash's stucco removed. In 1928 Mrs Ethel Morris lived at the hall. She was the daughter of the Reverend George Boughey and had married John Robert Morris in 1919. In 1956 Aqualate passed to her sister, Eva, who had married John Wollaston Greene, and in 1973 to her niece Celina Juhre.

Above: Aqualate Hall. Below: This rather pleasant painting shows Nash's dramatic design of Aqualate. Opposite page: The house in 1686 (Plot)

Ash Hall, Ash Bank, Werrington

Nursing Home

Ash Hall was built in 1837 for Job Meigh, an earthenware manufacturer, of the firm of Hicks, Meigh and Shelton. Meigh had purchased Ash House and its adjoining estate and built the hall on it. (1) The hall was built from local red sandstone in a Gothic Revival style. It had tall mullioned windows and a gabled façade embellished with stone pinnacles and miniature turrets. Over the portico are heraldic arms and a motto “Benigno Humine”. The interior was lavishly fitted with ornamental ceilings and pseudo-Elizabethan rafters. (2) Standing in a park with islands of trees the hall had black and gold entrance gates, flanked by monkey puzzle trees.

Job Meigh died at Ash Hall in 1862 and his wife in 1870. Their son, William, who was a widower then moved into the hall. William Meigh died six years later when his son, also William moved from Clayton Hall. This William, his wife Anita and their three children are listed on the 1881 census at Ash Hall where they employed four domestic servants. William Meigh died in 1922. In 1986, a survey of buildings by the Department of the Environment described Ash Hall as a large house built in a Tudor/Flemish/Gothic style. The main front was symmetrical and comprised two tall storeys with gable-lit attics. Slightly projecting gabled wings, with three sided bay windows, placed centrally, rose to two storeys with stone mullioned and transomed lights. The first floor central recess had a moulded band running across to the gables and a central stepped three-light window. The bands formed a cornice to a widely projecting single-storey porch, which has octagonal miniature turrets at angles rising to domed pinnacles.

In 1925 the estate was broken up and sold. The hall was acquired by a builder who converted it into The Ash Hall Golf Links Hotel. He added a spacious ballroom and the park and adjoining fields became a golf course.

Ash Hall was converted to a country club in 1939 and during World War II it was occupied by Cassel hospital, which had been evacuated from Kent. In 1946 it was acquired by Parker’s Brewery as an hotel and by 1952 it was the main office of Lawley pottery group which became part of Allied English Potteries. In the 1970s it was the local headquarters of the Opencast Executive of the National Coal Board. Ash Hall became a nursing home for the elderly in 1992.

The entrance (west) front

Above: The south front
Bottom left: The entrance front from the south
Bottom right: The inscription and arms over the main entrance

Ashenhurst Hall, Bradnop, Leek

Demolished

A house owned by John Ashenhurst was taxed for four hearths in 1666, which may have been the original house. In c. 1745, a new house designed by Joseph Sanderson was built for William Stanley. The house faced east and had an irregular plan, which was partly concealed by symmetrical elevations on the north and east, giving it the appearance of a double-pile house. It is probable that the earlier house survived behind the new elevations. The principal elevation was of seven bays with Corinthian pilasters at each end. The three central bays projected and were surmounted by a pediment. There were plantations around the house and a landscaped park to the north and east. Scrivener and Sons of Hanley remodelled the north side of the house in 1910. (1)

William Stanley had inherited Ashenhurst Hall in 1744 from his uncle Thomas Hollinshead, the son of Francis Hollinshead. Francis's father, also Francis, had purchased the Ashenhurst estate from his cousin John Ashenhurst in 1667. The house built by William Stanley passed down until in 1772, Lawrence Stanley left the estate to his sister Frances, wife of Reverend George Salt. (2)

Ashenhurst was offered for sale in the July 1794 edition of the *Derby Mercury*: "Sale by Private Contract of Ashenhurst with demesne land, an ancient water corn mill and several farms totaling upwards of 800 acres of arable, pasture, meadow and wood. Also a mansion house with good gardens, pleasure grounds, coach houses and stabling. The estate was said to be near lime, well watered and to abound with fish and game. Situated 2 miles from Leek and 12 miles from Ashbourne." The house failed to sell and remained in the possession of the Salts. An entry in John Sneyd's diary in 1807 records a visit by the Sneyds to Mrs Salt at Ashenhurst. Frances Salt left Ashenhurst to her god-daughter Margaret Leigh who sold it in 1824 to Richard Badnall of Highfield Hall near Leek for £17,550. He was a local silk dyer in Leek.

Badnall spent several thousand pounds on improving the buildings but to no avail for he was declared bankrupt in 1826 and a sale was held at Ashenhurst in 1827 to dispose of "the whole of the valuable effects". On offer were lofty mahogany four posters, winged wardrobes, moreen curtains, a sarcophagus, turkey carpets, two fine-toned flutes, and other items too numerous to mention. The sale brochure describes Ashenhurst as recently modernised and embellished at great expense.

The estate comprised in excess of 319 acres, which included rich arable land, meadow, pasture and woodland. The sale also included a corn mill and a valuable stone quarry. The house was of three storeys, the principal storey had a spacious entrance hall, paved with dotted stone and finished with enriched cornice and ceiling. The drawing room (30 x 22 ft) had elegant bow windows to the floor, opening on to the lawn. An excellent dining room contained a Venetian window, a recess for a sideboard, and an Italian marble chimney piece with Doric columns. The ground floor also boasted a breakfast parlour, housekeeper's room, butler's pantry, manservant's room, store closet, kitchen, scullery and larder. Six principal bedrooms were situated on the first floor together with a library or music room, two dressing rooms, a water closet and a china closet.

The attic storey had eight bedchambers. In the basement were wine vaults and cellary (*sic*) for malt liquors. Outside was a large paved yard with a knife house, poultry house, bottle house, coal pen, dust hole, a drying ground and a large kitchen garden. The sale also included two coach houses, harness room, a six stall stable, a gentleman's lathe and work room, a four stall stable, a cow house for six beasts, thrashing barn, bullock house for twelve, a hay barn and a three stall stable for agricultural horses. Ashenhurst was surrounded by a park with plantations, an ornamental stream of water and was well stored with game. (Sale catalogue at Stafford Record Office.)

In June 1828 Ashenhurst and 143 acres were sold to Samuel and William Phillips who were brothers and Leek silk manufacturers. They also owned Field House, now the National Reserve Club in High Street, Leek (see p.69. White's *Directory of Staffordshire* of 1851 records Ashenhurst as "the pleasant seat of S & W Phillips, Esquires". The estate was inherited by a nephew, Captain Thomas Phillips and then by his daughter Elsie Boynton. It was her son Thomas who demolished Ashenhurst in 1954. The stable block survives.

It was situated south of the railway line and the cross-roads on the A523.

SALES BY

Messrs. Barnes & Thornton.

THE COSTLY EFFECTS

Of Mr. BADNALL, Jun. ASHENHURST HALL,

Elegant Household Furniture, Upright Grand Piano Forte, Service of Plate, Linen, Library of Books, Original Paintings, Wines, China, Glass, Fixtures, Steam Kitchen, Farming Stock, Pair of Carriage Horses, Saddle Ditto, Dennett Chaise, Milch Cows, Sporting Dogs, Fowling Pieces, Lathe, Rare Plants, Erection of Kennel, Gear of Water Mill, Iron Fencing, and various valuable Effects.

LEEK, STAFFORDSHIRE.

TO BE SOLD BY AUCTION,

BY MESSRS. BARNES & THORNTON,

On the Premises, Ashenhurst Hall, Leek, on WEDNESDAY, FEBRUARY 14th, 1827, and three following days, at Ten o'Clock, by Order of the Assigness of Messrs. Badnall, Spilsbury, and Cruso ;

THE Whole of the VALUABLE EFFECTS at Ashenhurst Hall, viz.

BED ROOM FURNITURE.—Lofty mahogany four post bedsteads and furnitures, bedding, winged wardrobes, chests of drawers, dressing stands, and all other bed chamber articles.

THE DINING ROOM AND LIBRARY FURNITURE.—Moreen curtains, patent dining tables, chairs, pedestal sideboard and sarcophagus, claw, trio, card, and library tables, couches, cabinets, bookcases, Turkey carpets, rugs, pair of eighteen-inch globes, two fine toned flutes, &c.

A SUPERFLUITY OF FURNITURE in Hall, Kitchens, and Servants Apartments : brewing utensils, live and dead stock, out-door articles, harness, carts, plough, boring rods, rollers, manure, garden utensils, &c. The whole of fixtures, ranges, stoves, tanks, pumps, lead and iron pipes, coppers, and numberless other items, too numerous to detail in an advertisement.

To be viewed two days prior to sale by Catalogues, to be had at one shilling each, at Ashenhurst Hall ; Red Lion, Leek ; Green Man, Ashbourn ; King's Head, Derby ; Grove, Buxton ; Hotel, Macclesfield ; Bridgewater Hotel, Manchester ; Buck, Newcastle ; Crown, Stone ; White Hart, Uttoxeter ; Lion and Swan, Congleton ; George, Knutsford ; Swan, Hanley ; Legs of Man, Burslem ; Star, Stafford ; and of Messrs. BARNES and THORNTON, Land Surveyors and Auctioneers, 33, Fenchurch-street, London.

Sale particulars for 1827

Above: Kean's sketch of the house

Below: The memorial to John Ashenhurst who died in 1597. He had four wives, four sons and six daughters, all portrayed with him. The memorial is in St Edward's Church, Leek

Ball Haye Hall, off Park Road, Leek

Demolished

A house called Ball Haye standing on this site in 1565 was granted to Henry Davenport. The ownership of the hall passed down through the Davenport family until John Davenport, a Leek lawyer, died in 1786. As John Davenport died childless his nephew James Hulme succeeded him. James was the son of John Davenport's sister Sarah and her husband James Hulme. The hall pictured overleaf was rebuilt by James Hulme who also purchased more land in 1807. Although James Hulme was living at Ball Haye in 1811 he lived elsewhere for much of his life. (1)

In March 1788 the *Derby Mercury* advertised for a tenant for Ball Haye Hall. The hall is described as the late residence of John Davenport, deceased. The hall was then tenanted by Colonel and Mrs Dobson who were often visited at the hall by the Sneyd family who joined them for regular "Oyster Meetings". Apparently these were occasions when friends met to eat oysters for breakfast. (2) In 1799 John Dobson paid £1.1s 0d Easter Dues for Ball Haye. (3)

The hall was the subject of a chancery suit for many years. The suit involved James Hulme and his wife Elizabeth and six of the children of Elizabeth by her first marriage. The house was let for several years before the appointed trustees offered it for sale in 1830 at the Red Lion in Leek. The sale notice in the *Macclesfield Courier* of 3rd April 1830 refers to the mansion house, pews in the church and cottages. The rooms on the ground floor of the hall comprised entrance hall; dining room; drawing room; breakfast room; study; housekeepers room; butlers room; servants hall; hot and cold baths, kitchen and other offices. On the upper floors were ten good lodging rooms; four dressing closets and adjoining lodging rooms for servants. Outside were pleasure grounds and shrubberies, 73 acres in all. The hall was not sold at this time, however. At the time of sale the hall was uninhabited, the previous tenant being Francis Gybbon Spilsbury, a Leek silk manufacturer.

In 1853 the hall and 43 acres was sold to Joshua and John Brough, they were nephews of James Hulme. In 1870 a lease was granted to Andrew Jukes Worthington for 14 years at an annual rent of £204.5s. He sub-leased the hall with its garden and grounds together with the plantation, the lake and island and 26 acres of parkland. The plantation had provided a resting place for Chartist rioters when they came to Leek in 1842. Andrew Worthington died in 1873 and his widow lived in the hall for some years. The hall was unoccupied in 1880 but Ernest Worthington, Andrew's son, lived there in 1881. Ernest and his wife Maude employed a housekeeper, two domestic servants and a groom at Ball Haye. John Hall leased Ball Haye from 1882 and lived there until he died in 1930. He is remembered by giving his name to John Hall's gardens, which were part of the grounds of the hall. Generations of Leek children have thrown bread to the ducks on the pond in the gardens. The pond is the lake and island leased to Andrew Worthington in 1870.

William Spooner Brough, John's son, the next owner of the hall, died unmarried in 1917 and left the property to his nephew H.H. Brindley. In 1913 W.S. Brough had given Leek Urban District Council ten and a half acres of his Ball Haye estate for use as a public park. Brindley sold the hall and 27 acres to the Trustees of the Leek Memorial Cottage Hospital in 1931. It was intended to build a new hospital in the grounds of the hall but this did not happen. The hall and its grounds were occupied by American Servicemen during World War II. With the introduction of the National Health Service, the hall passed from the trustees to the NHS, along with the funds collected for the new hospital.

The hall was used as a Polish Club from 1946 but later was converted into flats. Pevsner describes the hall as comprising seven bays and being three storeys high. It was ashlar faced and had a doorway with unfluted Roman Doric columns and triglyph frieze. By the 1970s the hall had become derelict and it was demolished in 1972. The site is occupied by the present Leisure Centre.

Ball Haye from Rev. Dr Nightingale's Description of the County of Stafford, c. 1808. Note the bay, later removed on the left side

A later view with additions to the east side of the house

Above: The house in the early 1960s

Below: Forlorn and deserted a decade later

Belmont Hall, Belmont Road, Ipstones

Reduced

This current house is included because it would appear to be the east wing only of a much larger building. It contains no stairwell of any substance which one would have expected. A little to the west is a lawn with known voids below it, which could have been cellars of another part of the house. There is a traditional tale told locally that the house once had a *porte-cochere* which could have been located between two wings. According to Rev. F. Brighton part of the mansion was dismantled after the Sneyd family moved to Basford and Ashcombe.

No early images of the house appear to have survived so quite a mystery remains. Maybe one day an excavation of the lawn will reveal more clues.

In 1878, it had nine pools within its grounds, of which at least three survive. The photograph shows the house as it is today. Belmont was built for John Sneyd in 1771, who died there in 1809. This may have been c. 1806 and after a fire.

At that time the gardens at Belmont were considered to be among the finest in England. In the early 1800s, John Sneyd had been awarded gold medals for the extensive wooded plantations he created there. His grandson Thomas was living at the hall by 1834 (1) and still owned it when White's Directory of 1851 described Belmont Hall as "the sylvan seat of Thomas Sneyd, surrounded by extensive woods". Thomas Sneyd, however, lived in Dawlish at this time (censuses 1851 and 1861). During the 1870s and 1880s Belmont was occupied by Mrs Sneyd-Kinnersley, but in 1896 it was unoccupied, the owner being Dryden Henry Sneyd, the great-grandson of John Sneyd. Dryden was still the owner in 1908 although John Richards tenanted the hall.

Indeed the Sneyd family owned Belmont Hall until 1913 when it was sold. Later residents of the hall include a Miss Slack, Thomas Scarratt, Charles Victor Shufflebotham and George Walker Collins. Mary Burnett Scarratt, daughter of Thomas of Belmont later became Lady Southwell. She owned Belmont in 1937 when C.V. Shufflebotham was the tenant. (2) In recent years, the Ball and Skellam families owned it, selling to John and Jodi Peck in 1974. They sold it in 1993 to Mr and Mrs Wheatley. This cadet branch of the Sneyd family also owned Ashcombe at Cheddleton, and Basford Hall, between Ashcombe and Belmont. Basford is still in the family, although not by direct line.

*Belmont today.
The rest of the house was to the left*

Beresford Hall – SW of Hartington

Demolished

South-west of Hartington was a Staffordshire estate adjoining Beresford Dale. For decades after its demolition, the OS maps showed its position, a reminder of reckless loss. However, the building destroyed in c. 1858 was only part of what had been a much larger building.

A painting of the house by Linnell and dated 1815 shows the house from the Upper Bowling Green. It shows the two wings fortunately from the south, i.e. from the rear of the photographs on p.34. The rear part – the building with three gables – was perhaps the earliest. It is similar to both Hartington Hall (1611) and Youlgreave Old Hall (panelling dated 1650 or 1656, but which may be older). It is not clear from the 1815 painting whether the two end gables projected, but the photograph of the ruins seems to suggest not.

The (apparent) later wing is more unusual for North Staffordshire and it is a pity it was demolished. The 1815 painting indicates that a two-storey extension existed on the rear elevation with a flat roof. It seems to have a parapet with stone balls on the top. The ancestral home of the Beresfords, the estate passed to Olive Stanhope in 1623. She was the granddaughter of Edward Beresford. Her husband, Charles Cotton, died in 1658, whereupon the estate passed to her son Charles, the celebrated author and poet. He was born at the house in 1630 and died in 1687. He sold the property in 1680; he is known to have had pressing creditors and may have been forced to sell. In 1666, the hall was assessed for six hearths in the Hearth Tax.

The reason why Charles Cotton was short of money could be because he was responsible for erecting the later building. His acquisition of the estate in 1658 would seem to fit the suggested date of construction in the VCH. The corbelled pediment over the entrance of the 'new' wing had a 'bear rampant' on a sheild, not visible (but there) on the upper photograph on p.34.

The purchaser was Joseph Woodhouse of Wolfscote, across the River Dove. A year later, it passed back into the Beresford family, when John Beresford of Newton Grange acquired it. The family connection ended again in 1723 when it passed to George Osborne, who was still there in 1739. Seven years later, it passed again, to Walter, Lord Aston. In 1825, William, Viscount Beresford purchased the estate and it remained in the family until 1901. The VCH (1) has an interesting section on the various owners (on which the above is based). Sleigh (2) has a family tree of the Beresfords showing that a descendant of Charles Cotton was the 7th Duke of Devonshire.

The rear portion was abandoned to the elements between 1815–38 but the south-fronted section continued in use as a farmhouse, being described as being "in tolerable order" in 1838. Twenty years later, it was pulled down by A.J. Beresford Hope, the stepson of Viscount Beresford (and his second cousin), with a view to rebuilding it. William Butterfield appears to have been the architect, but the plans came to nothing. Beresford Hope was a founder member of the influential Cambridge Camden Society, which promoted a return to the construction of churches on medieval principles.

The tower in the grounds, close to the river, but on an outcrop above it, was rebuilt from the walls of its cellar, all that remained in 1905. The work was undertaken by F.W. Green of York, who acquired the estate in 1901. It may be seen to advantage from the lane which runs along the length of Wolfscote Hill and (in winter) from Mill Lane, Hartington. Also surviving is the Fishing House built by Charles Cotton in 1674.

Above: The west front. It was adjoined by a wing at the rear of the left-hand side

Below: The rear wing which collapsed between 1815-38

Above: The west wing (to the right), with the earlier south facing block behind it. From 'The Beresfords of Beresford'

Below: A rare view of the house from the south, showing the west wing and the (?older) building at the rear. This view is from the Upper Bowling Green and is dated 1815

Charles Cotton's Fishing Lodge or Temple. It is dated 1674

Betley Hall, Betley

Demolished

George Tollet (born 1696) bought a hall in 1718 from a branch of the Egerton family. The hall had an interesting stained glass window featuring Morris Dancers. The Tollets settled in Betley and continued to live in the village for two centuries. (1) This original Betley Hall, a half-timbered building, later became Old Hall Farm. In 1780, Charles Tollet built a new hall at Betley which he estimated would cost £3,000, (2). This new hall, pictured below, was a fine, three- storey Georgian building with gardens and a picturesque lake. By 1851, another family member, George Tollet, lived there with his five adult children, his daughter-in-law, granddaughter and fourteen servants. The staff included a Swiss governess for the ten-year-old granddaughter. George Tollet died in 1855 and with his death the importance of Betley Hall diminished. Six years later the Tollets no longer lived at the hall; it was occupied by Samuel Hope, a magistrate, with his wife and two young children. Betley Hall, however, was still owned by the Tollet family. Kelly's *Post Office Directory* of 1860 described it as the seat of Charles Wicksted, Esq but it was tenanted by Samuel Pearce Hope. In 1814 a Charles Tollet had changed his surname to Wicksted to satisfy the terms of his maternal great-uncle's will. The hall was tenanted by Francis Broade in 1872 but by 1881 Charles' son, George Wicksted, was living there. George died in 1895 and his widow, Margaret, married Col. J.A. Macdonald. They continued to live at the hall until the 1920s. The estate was then sold and divided. Betley Hall gradually fell into a state of disrepair and by 1980 all that remained was the crumbling remains of the shell of the entrance hall (3).

Betley Hall from the lake, "the seat of George Tollet"

Biddulph Grange, Biddulph

Apartments

In 1812, James Bateman Esq of Knypersley Hall bought the title of the vicarage called the Grange; three years later he acquired Woodhouse Farm and Poolfields and formed the nucleus of the Grange estate. (1) James Bateman, son of John Bateman of Knypersley Hall, moved from Knypersley to Biddulph Grange in 1842. The Grange was at this time an old farmhouse surrounded by swampy ground on a bleak hillside. (2)

The old farmhouse was demolished and James Bateman built a large, stone mansion in an Italianate Renaissance style. He laid out a varied garden including an Egyptian court, a Chinese ground and an Italian garden. They are still a prime document of early Victorian garden layout. Members of the Bateman family continued to live here until the Grange was offered for sale in 1871.

The sale catalogue of 1871 described Biddulph Grange as a handsome, commanding and well-arranged building of sandstone (the upper part being cemented over) in the semi-Italianate style. The ground floor included entrance hall, inner hall, dining room, map room, anteroom, library, oak room, breakfast room, smoking room, billiard room, picture gallery, geological gallery, main gallery, studio and conservatory. The upper floors contained a gallery, a boudoir, fourteen principal bedroom and sixteen other bedrooms for bachelors and servants. In addition there were large kitchens, outbuildings, stables, carriage houses, a granary, blacksmith's shop, joiner's shop and storerooms.

It was bought by Robert Heath II, a wealthy industrialist, who made additions and improvements, adding a new wing at a cost of £20,000. At the time of the 1881 census James Heath, an ironmaster, who was unmarried, aged 29, lived here with his younger brother and two younger sisters. Their staff enjoyed a certain hierarchy as there are first, second and third housemaids and first and second footmen. A housekeeper, cook, kitchen and scullery maids completed the staff.

In 1896 the house caught fire and was almost destroyed. At the time the Heath family and most of the staff were residing at Greenway Bank while extensions to the Grange were being undertaken. (3) In August 1896 the *Congleton Chronicle* reported, "the new grange, future home of Mr. Robert Heath of Greenway Bank, is progressing satisfactorily".

Biddulph Grange was sold in 1921 to Lancashire County Council for use as a children's orthopaedic hospital and a new wing was added at a cost of £60,000. It later became part of the Birmingham Regional Hospital Board.

In 1988 the National Trust acquired the gardens at Biddulph Grange and after extensive restoration opened them to the public. Recently a four-bedroomed apartment situated within Biddulph Grange Mansion with views over the National Trust Gardens was offered for rental at a cost of £2,500 per month.

The house from the garden

The tower from the Chinese garden

Another part of the Chinese garden

Biddulph Old Hall, Biddulph

Ruins

Little remains today of what must have been a fascinating house, although there is a twist in the tale of its history. Construction is thought to be of c. 1560, although the only part dated is from 1580, on the southern entrance. Built of local stone, with large bay windows, it must have been a fine property, with four fronts around a rectangular courtyard.

However, the house was caught up in the Civil War and reduced to a shell by Parliamentary forces. Today the only walls that survive are those on the external side of the house, although they give a flavour of what the house must have looked like. (1) It was not a fortified manor house but built for comfort rather than sieges although it had five portholes for cannon let into parts of the west wall and lower chamber of the tower. (2) The ruins of Biddulph Hall were offered for sale in 1871. (3) The catalogue described four partially destroyed walls with square mullioned windows. An entrance porch and an ivy-clad cupola-roofed tower were thought to add ample interest to the sale. The 'mansion', also included in the sale, had twelve rooms with a two-stall stable and saddle room outside.

The recent twist in the story concerns the house that remained on the site after the rest of the property was demolished. For centuries it had been assumed that it had been built on the site after the Civil War. Purchased recently and refurbished, it was found from tree-ring dating to be older, not younger, than the old hall. After considerable expense, it is now secured for a much extended life and at long last appreciated for its antiquity. This property featured on a BBC TV programme in 2005. The owners wished to restore the tower that survived of the Old Hall, but from which all the floors had been removed. Despite concern over its stability, a protracted debate on its restoration seemed to be risking its future.

Three views (above and overleaf) taken c. 100 years ago of the ruined house

Blythe House, Blythe Bridge

Demolished

Charles Harvey, a pottery manufacturer and banker who lived at Longton Hall, (see p105) built Blythe House in 1853. This large house was Tudor in style with a tower at one end. Buttressed walls housed a number of bay windows and several tall chimney stacks surmounted the house. A large entrance hall led to morning, dining and drawing rooms and a grand staircase rose to seven bedrooms, a dressing room, saloon and linen room. A courtyard at the rear of the house had stables, a coach house, potting house and a laundry. Blythe House stood in grounds and gardens extending to sixteen acres. When Charles Harvey died in 1860 his son William Kenwright Harvey inherited the estate. William was not an astute businessman and his inefficiency led to the bank failing. William disappeared with the gold from the bank, leaving debts of £40,000. The creditors eventually received five shillings in the pound. In 1866 the house and contents were sold at public auction. George Bennion lived at Blythe House in the early 20th century; he was an alderman of the borough of Longton and had been Lord Mayor of Longton on four occasions. (1) A later occupant of the house was T.C. Wild, the Longton pottery manufacturer. Blythe House was demolished in 1939. The library, a police station and a row of houses now stand on the site.

The entrance front & tower

Butterton Hall, nr Newcastle-Under-Lyme
Demolished

The Old Hall was built in 1540 by William Swynnerton (sic) and was still standing in 1844. It was a red, sandstone built manor house. According to a report by the North Staffordshire Field Club in 1944 just scanty remains could be seen. This Tudor, castellated hall was of three storeys and had mullioned windows and large chimney stacks. The hall passed from Thomas Swinnerton to Lady Pilkington.

Sir William Pilkington, Bart., who died in 1850, built the new hall near the site of the old hall, in 1847. This elegant, stone house in a Revived Gothic style had a tower over the porch and turrets. Lady Pilkington continued to live at the hall after her husband's death. The hall was tenanted, in 1884, by Capt. George Shakerley and in 1908 by Robert Lewis Johnson, although it was still owned by the Pilkington family.

After being used by the military, during World War I, it fell into disrepair and, apart from the stable block, was demolished in 1924. Some of the stone from the hall was used in local buildings including the clubhouse at Newcastle Golf Club.

Butterton Hall in 1847 as rebuilt in Gothic Revival style. It was then the seat of Sir William Pilkington

Two views of the previous hall from Shaw (1798)

Calwich Abbey, Ellastone

Demolished

Prior to its dissolution, Calwich was occupied by the Black Canons. It was purchased in 1543 from the king by John Fleetwood of a family from Lancashire. A descendant, Sir Richard Fleetwood, built nearby Wootton Lodge, one of the finest houses in the county. The estate was sold to Bernard Granville in 1738. He built a house to the east of the site of the 1847 house (see opposite top), which indicates that the former was on the floodplain of the Dove, or just above it. He also widened the river to produce a lake and made extensive improvements to the gardens and landscape.

Granville had two sisters, the celebrated diarist Mrs Delany and Mrs Ann Dewes. The former's diary has some interesting detail on the Calwich garden: (1)

"She (Mrs Delany) and Ann had given him (Bernard) much advice as to the layout of the garden and the furnishing of the house. Bernard had inherited the fortune of Lord Lansdowne, their uncle and their father's brother." Mrs Delany had visited Norwood Park, Thoresby and Worksop and wrote: "Much magnificence I have seen in this country; lawns, vast woods, palaces of houses, but nothing so pretty as Calwich." In 1756, Ann wrote to her brother, saying, "Your garden it is said to outdo any of the wonders of the Peak. Mrs Hayes, who has just returned from Mrs FitzHerberts (?Tissington or Norbury Manor) says Calwich is reputed by everyone to be much the prettiest place in the two counties of Stafford and Derbyshire."

Granville was a friend of Handel and it is held locally that his *Water Music* was inspired by the lake at Calwich and possibly even written in the surviving summer house by the lake. Handel was to leave a folio of his music in his will to his host. Another visitor was J.J. Rousseau, when he was living at Wootton. Granville was the only local person with whom he could converse in French. In July 1774, Mary Dewes, the daughter of Ann, married John Port of Ilam Hall. Bernard died at Calwich in 1776 and is interred in the Granville Vault in St Peter's Church, Ellastone. When he died he left Calwich to his sister Ann's third son John Dewes (also spelt D'ewes). She had married a John Dewes in 1740.

In the 1830s, the house was owned by Court Dewes. During the 1830s, Dewes lived at The Grey House in Church Street, Ashbourne, which may indicate that Calwich was let at the time. In 1846, the Hon. and Rev. Augustus Duncombe purchased the estate. *The Staffordshire Advertiser* reported on 3rd April 1847 that the house was to be demolished "having commenced the erection of a new residence, on a more commanding and healthy site". In 1908, Major Alfred Charles Duncombe JP, son of Augustus, was the proprietor and occasional resident of this new house. (2)

The estate was put up for sale on 1st July 1926. However, the house survived until 1935, when it was demolished, a rear wing only surviving. The year 1935 also saw the loss of nearby Wootton Hall and Ilam Hall. The ornate garden wall featured on the photograph (see page 48 top) survives at Red Oakes, Rea Cliffe Road, Rudyard, near Leek, having been purchased at the demolition sale by Wardle Sales, a dyer of Leek.

Fortunately, a drawing of the Granville house survives. It appears in *Ashbourne and the Valley of the Dove*, published in 1839, reproduced (opposite).

Above: Bernard Granville's house; it was situated below its replacement of 1847

Below: The west or entrance front to the Duncombe house

Above: The south front of the Duncombe House

Below: The north-west portion of the house. There are two wings here, with the rear one (part of which survived demolition of the house in 1935) looking less weathered and perhaps dating after the 1840s. Compare with p 47 (top)

Above: The east front of the main house and the north-east wing
Below: The east front, facing the valley and lake

Above: Another view of the east front; outbuildings stretch behind the tree to the right

Below: The Lodge, Dove Street, Ellastone

Viewed from the lake, this view shows just how substantial the property was

Clayton Hall, Newcastle-Under-Lyme

School

Pevsner described Clayton Hall as probably Georgian with Italianate contributions of the 1840s. He described a rendered building with a central block with giant angle pilasters and a lantern over the centre. This replaced an old, low-gabled hall built in the 16th or early 17th century (see below), the new hall was built on a site further east in the 1840s. It was the home of John Ashford Wise, a magistrate and M.P. for Stafford. In 1851 this wealthy man employed a number of servants to cater for the needs of himself, his wife, Mary Ann, and their three young children. The children had a governess and a nurse and Mary Ann Wise had her own lady's maid as well as the housekeeper, housemaid and butler she needed to maintain her household. White's *Directory* of 1851 described Clayton Hall as a large white mansion, pleasantly situated.

Lovat Wise, son of John, lived at Clayton Hall in 1881. He was an officer in the Staffordshire Yeomanry and a county J.P. Lovat seems to have introduced a hierarchy into his staff as he employed both a nurse and under-nurse as well as a housemaid and an under-housemaid. Two lady's maids were in residence at the hall on the night of the census, presumably one for the lady of the house and the other for her sister who was visiting.

By 1896 the hall was occupied by Frederick Johnson. Members of the Johnson family, who were pottery manufacturers, owned it until 1940. It was requisitioned by the Admiralty and used as a training centre for the Fleet Air Arm and known as HMS *Daedalus*. (1) In 1948 the hall became a girls grammar school. (2)

The old low-gabled hall

Clough Hall, Kidsgrove

Demolished

The site of Clough Hall has been occupied for over 400 years. Clough House is mentioned in 1583 as the ancestral home of the Unwyn family. In the 1640s John Unwyn demolished this first house and built The Clough.

This was probably demolished in 1800 and replaced by the fine Georgian mansion pictured overleaf, built by John Gilbert, junior, and set in grounds of 126 acres with stables, kitchen gardens, ornamental walks and a lake. His father John Gilbert, senior, agent for the Duke of Bridgewater, had purchased this estate in about 1782.

On the death of Gilbert in 1812, the property was put up for auction at the Roebuck Inn, Newcastle-under-Lyme on 30th December of that year. The hall is described as a magnificent stone structure well calculated for the residence of a large, genteel family. A central pediment to the roof, a portico supported by four plain Roman columns over the main entrance, two dining rooms, two drawing rooms and a breakfast room are mentioned plus thirteen bedrooms. It reputedly sold in 1813 for £64,000 to Thomas Kinnersley, a banker from Newcastle-under-Lyme. Thomas, who had lived at Chesterton Hall, moved in sometime after this. His son, also Thomas, took over the entire estate in 1819, developing a mine and ironworks in nearby Kidsgrove. Thomas entertained lavishly, many guests passing down his immaculate carriageway past ornamental lodges to enjoy elaborate meals, hunting, walks through the grounds and boating on his lake.The 1851 census shows that Thomas and his wife Mary employed ten house servants. Thomas Kinnersley died, rich and respected in 1855 and his widow, Mary, continued to live at Clough Hall until her death in 1877. She continued to keep a large staff including footman, coachman and pageboy.

CLOUGH HALL PARK AND GARDENS.
KIDSGROVE AND HARECASTLE STATIONS.

OPEN WET OR FINE.

130 ACRES LIGHTED BY ELECTRICITY!

Shelter for 20,000 people.

IMPORTANT NOTICE!

"BEAUTIFUL VENICE."
MONDAYS, THURSDAYS AND SATURDAYS ONLY.

In consequence of its undoubted success, and in compliance with the wishes of many visitors, the Directors have decided to give
THREE GRAND ILLUMINATED PERFORMANCES
ON MONDAY, THURSDAY AND SATURDAY EVENINGS,
AT 7-30 OF THE
THE GRAND OPEN-AIR SPECTACLE.
"BEAUTIFUL VENICE."

BALLET OF 200 LADIES.
GORGEOUS DRESSES.

The attention of the General Public is drawn to the important fact, The LAST WEEK of the Grandest Open-air Production ever seen.

POSITIVELY THE LAST PERFORMANCES.

Every Evening this Week.
VARIETY ENTERTAINMENT IN LARGE PAVILION
By Talented Artistes, concluding with a Farcical Comedy, entitled—
"THE AREA BELLE."
MILITARY AND ORCHESTRAL BANDS DAILY.
D A N C I N G
ON TWO LARGE PLATFORMS.

VENETIAN MANDOLIN SERENADERS, AND WATER PARTIES.

COMIC WATER CARNIVAL

MAGNIFICENT DOUBLE DISPLAY OF FIREWORKS,

Monday, Thursday, and Saturday.

Steam Launch and Rowing Boats on Large Lake; Fishing, Shooting, Switchback Railway, Ærial Flight, Patent Swings, New Monkey House, Bowling Green; Cricket Ground, Bicycle Track, and numerous other amusements,

ADMISSION SIXPENCE,

"BEAUTIFUL VENICE" AND ALL ENTERTAINMENTS FREE,

CHEAP RAILWAY FARES FROM ALL PARTS.

LATE TRAINS BACK,

The Clough Hall Park and garden advertising its attractions

After a period of neglect the mansion was sold to the Biddulph iron magnate, Robert Heath for about £10,000, and much of the estate for a further £24,000. Heath sold on the house to a consortium of Manchester businessmen (reputedly for £33,000) who aimed to convert it and the grounds into a pleasure resort on the lines of Belle Vue, Manchester. When it was opened at Whitsun 1890, it was billed as the largest pleasure garden in the country. A pavilion had been built for refreshments and stage shows, which could hold 5,000 people standing or 3,500 seated. An outdoor dancing platform "on which 2,000 couples can disport themselves with ease" was later joined by another of equal size. There were also on offer various sports – cricket, archery, athletics, bowls, fairground rides, a conservatory and monkey house, boating and swimming on two lakes and a captive balloon, from which regular parachute jumps were made. The opening day featured Blondin on the high wire, four brass bands and a ladies' cricket match topped off by a firework display.

Later attractions at "The Paradise of the Potteries" included "*Beautiful Venice*" a musical extravaganza involving 150 colourfully costumed dancers and twelve gondoliers on specially built canals.

This enterprise lasted until 1907, after which the Hall became a public house and was used by Belgian refugees during Word War I. Upkeep became a problem and the Hall was demolished in 1927, part of the grounds becoming a public park.

(Information based on notes at Kidsgrove Library, largely by Philip Leese, a local historian.)

Clough Hall from the lake

Consall Hall, Consall

Remodelled

Situated above the Churnet Valley, this house was built in brick in 1809 by Edward Leigh. Following the bankruptcy of John Leigh in 1845, the house was offered for sale with "about 2,000 acres" as an investment by the mortgagees. No buyer was possibly found, for it was later sold in 1849. The house had been let for seven years in 1841, so the mortgagees clearly waited until they could sell with vacant possession. It was then purchased by the Hyde-Smiths. It was later sold in 1892 to James Henry Meakin. He died in 1915 and the house was sold in 1918 to William and Alberta Podmore, having been vacant. At that time the view from the house was foreshortened, both by shrubs and trees, but also by a pit heap: colliery waste from Ladypark Colliery. Mine shafts existed behind the house and also to the south. William Podmore's son, also called William (the present owner), together with his late wife Edna, transformed the dereliction and industrial wasteland into a fantastic 70-acre landscape garden, removing the pit heaps and 450,000 (sic) tons of spoil in the process. The story of the development of this amazing garden has recently been published. (1)

The house was formerly much larger. In 1959, the present owner reduced it by removing thirteen rooms and five kitchens. It had been built with two span roofs and a central valley. The main entrance, facing south and situated on the gable (the Garden Front) has been moved to the west side, giving access to a stairwell housing the oak staircase from Wootton Hall. This was purchased at the demolition sale in 1935, along with the front wall of Rousseau's Cave, now re-erected in the terrace below the south front. The former twin gabled roof was replaced by a single span, hidden behind a brick pediment. On the west side of the house there used to be a small addition visible on a photograph (see p.56b). This was the Eagle House. Did it once contain these fine birds, perhaps in Victorian times?

James Meakin's brother purchased Westwood Hall, west of Consall, on 29th August 1871 for £41,500. The estate extended to 828 acres and had been sold by the Executors of the late Capt. Powis. (2) (see p.154)

Consall Hall garden is open to the public on Wednesdays, Sundays and Bank Holiday Mondays, 10am – 5pm.

The house today, set in a magnificent garden extending to over 70 acres

Above: Consall Hall prior to redevelopment in the 1960s. The entrance was on the gabled garden front

Below: The former garden front and entrance, with what may have been the Eagle House on the left

STAFFORDSHIRE.

MOST IMPORTANT AND

Valuable Estates,

SUCH AS SELDOM ARE BROUGHT INTO THE MARKET, with an

Inexhaustible extent of very superior Coal;

CAPITAL AND EXTENSIVE

FLINT AND POTTERY MILLS, LIME-KILNS,

RAILROADS, &c.

Offering an influential and first-rate Investment for any great Capitalist, and also a fine and beautiful Estate for Residence, with

Mansion, Manor, Woods, Plantations, and Fishery.

PARTICULARS

OF THE FINE AND TRULY IMPORTANT

FREEHOLD ESTATES

OF

CONSALL and WOODHEAD,

A short distance from the Towns of CHEADLE and LEEK,

AND ONLY EIGHTEEN MILES FROM BUXTON,

Tithe-free, extra-parochial, and exonerated of Land-Tax, except a very small portion,

WITH

THE MANOR OF CONSALL, WELL STOCKED WITH GAME, FISHERY,

Beautiful Woods, stored with thriving Oak, and

SEVERAL VALUABLE FARMS

SURROUNDING THE

MANSION OF CONSALL-HALL,

IN ALL

About Two Thousand Acres,

Partly bounded by the River Churnet and the Trent and Mersey Canal;

Within a few Miles of ALTON TOWERS, the splendid Seat of the EARL OF SHREWSBURY;

WHICH WILL BE SOLD BY AUCTION, BY

Messrs. DANIEL SMITH & SON,

By direction of the Mortgagees, under a Power of Sale,

AT THE MART, NEAR THE BANK OF ENGLAND,

On TUESDAY, the 26th day of AUGUST, 1845,

AT TWELVE O'CLOCK, IN TWO LOTS,

Unless an acceptable Offer shall be previously made by Private Contract.

Added to the great many recommendations of this fine Property is the incalculable value of the

MINERALS, about 1600 Acres,

Containing ascertained Strata or Mines of *superior Coal*, part already worked, and *VEINS of IRON-STONE*,

WITH RAILROADS COMPLETED TO THE CANAL AND TURNPIKE-ROADS;

Also, at a desirable distance from the Residence, several

VERY CAPITAL FLINT AND POTTERY MILLS, LIME-WORKS, &c.

Most substantially and admirably constructed, chiefly of Stone and Iron, with an immense Power of Water;

STONE QUARRIES AND WHARFS;

The Rental and estimated Value of the Property is about

£6000 per Annum,

WITH GREAT PROSPECTIVE INCREASE.

Particulars, with Plans, and every information may be obtained of Messrs. JENKYNS & PHELPS, Solicitors, 14, Red Lion-Square; at the Mart; at the chief Inns at Birmingham, Liverpool, Manchester, Stafford, Stone, Cheadle, Shrewsbury, and Wolverhampton; of Mr. EDWIN HEATON, of Leek; and of Messrs. DANIEL SMITH & SON, Land-Agents, in Waterloo-Place, Pall-Mall, where Plans may be inspected.

NORRIS AND SON, PRINTERS, BLOMFIELD-STREET, FINSBURY-CIRCUS.

The sale particulars of 1845

Cotton Hall, Cotton

Empty (former school)

The original building on this site may have been built by the Morrice family in 1630. Peter Lead reported that a stone lintel from the original house could be seen in the cellar of Cotton Hall in 1989. It had the inscription "WM 1630 EM". (1)

It became the home of Thomas Gilbert Snr and his son, also Thomas, inherited it in 1742. The latter was a land agent to the Marquis of Stafford and an MP for over 30 years. With his brother John, they introduced James Brindley to the Duke of Bridgewater and were early industrial entrepreneurs. The house seems to have been rebuilt in the late 18th century, prior to Thomas's death in 1798. The estate passed to his eldest son, the Rev. Thomas Gilbert, who held it until his death in 1841. The latter did not live there and the hall continued as the home of his stepmother, Mary, until her death in 1810.

Peter Lead outlines its remaining years under the Gilberts (2). After Mary's death, the house was let to a Mr Errington. The hall and estate was offered on a fourteen year lease from 1818. (3) On the Rev. Thomas's death (1814), the estate passed to a nephew, yet another Thomas, who died in 1843. The latter's widow put the property up for sale on 20th August 1845 at Cheadle. It consisted of the hall, stabling for twelve horses, plus "Gardener's House", Ice House, Bath House and Bath, Agricultural Buildings and Bailiff's House, the advowson of the adjacent Cotton Chapel and 338 acres of land. The *Macclesfield Courier* in 1839 announced the death, at Bath, of Richard Badnall, late of Cotton Hall.

Lead goes on to reveal that the purchaser was the 16th Earl of Shrewsbury, who purchased Cotton as a residence for his nephew and heir, Bertram. However, in 1846 he seems to have changed his mind. This may be because he had decided to use the talents of A.W.N. Pugin to rebuild Alton Castle, work which commenced in 1847. This would appear to have been for his nephew or possibly his wife upon being widowed. As a result, the Earl, a Roman Catholic, offered Cotton to Frederick William Faber and the Brothers of the Will of God. Pugin was also commissioned to build a church and extensions to the house, in 1846-48. The church was opened on 25th April 1848.

The diary of A.S. Bolton reveals that on 19th November, 1863, he went to a sale at Cotton Hall and bought "table etc" there. On 7th November 1865, he went to the sale of the Cotton Hall Estate at Derby. Only Lot 2 was sold, purchased by Charles Bill for £2,400. Lot 2 consisted of a farm and land on the east side of the road running north just east of the hall. The school wanted adjacent land for the benefit of its pupils – it had very little land other than some woodland, kitchen garden etc. However, the school withdrew bidding for Lot 2 at £2,250. The hall was not for sale, it was the ancillary land purchased by the Earl in 1845 and put on the market by trustees of his successor's estate.

Lots 1 and 3, being withdrawn from the auction, became the subject of a bid by A.S. Bolton shortly afterwards. However the lots were offered to the school and despite an uphill struggle were purchased for £12,000, completion being 1st June 1866.

Cotton Hall became a preparatory school for Sedgley Park in 1868 and the school moved to Cotton in 1873.

A.W.N. Pugin had died in 1852: his son was therefore sought to design extensions for the new school (development having awaited purchase of the land for playing fields etc). A shortage of capital saw development confined to a dormitory for 50 boys above the second floor of the old hall and the clock cloister, the latter built with two more dormitories above it. (4) The college continued their occupation until July 1987. In 1989, it was being developed into a hotel, conference and leisure complex (5) but this does not appear to have materialised. At the time of writing, the college premises, including the hall, are unoccupied.

A fascinating (and true) story of the days of the Gilberts and their 19th century relatives can be recounted; it relates to the tenancy of George Whieldon: "On Wednesday 12th May 1830 a loaded gun was fired at George Whieldon, a local magistrate, through his study window as he sat working late at night. He was hit in the face but not badly injured." A reward of £200, a huge amount, was offered for information. He had clearly upset someone, either on or off the bench! (6)

Right: The original chapel of 1795, now the parish church

Below: Cotton Hall, with its chapel

Above: The Gilbert house with mid-19th century additions to left and right, added by the Catholic school

Below: The house (mid photo) with later adjoining additions designed by A.W.N. Pugin's son

Crakemarsh Hall, Crakemarsh, Uttoxeter

Demolished

Pevsner (1) describes this house as being c. 1820, but with hints of it being rebuilt, particularly around a 17th century chestnut and oak staircase. The latter is described as being "sumptuous". It occupied the whole of the entrance hall, with "lavish openwork panels of acanthus foliage set between big square newels decorated with fruit and carrying urns of flowers". In fact the original house was built around or refaced; it was not demolished. The rooms are described as being "chastely Victorian" with some older "bits and pieces" which included a bolection-moulded marble fireplace and a back staircase with simple turned balusters both of which were early 18th century.

In c. 1789, Brian Hodgson moved here from Wootton Lodge, formerly of The Grey House, situated next to the old grammar school in Ashbourne, and recalled on a plaque in the nearby St Oswald's church. He was a senior partner in Charles Roe and Co of Macclesfield, who were copper and brass manufacturers of some importance. (2) He had earlier been the landlord of the Buxton Hall Hotel.

After the suppression of Croxden Abbey, Crakemarsh was held by Lord Burghersh, then the family of Delves and then Lord Sheffield, whose descendant sold it to his brother, Christopher Sheffield. It was then purchased by Gilbert Collier, whose son sold it to Sir Gilbert Gerard, Master of the Rolls. It was in the Gerard family for many years, later passing to the Cottons. Celia Fiennes passed the house in 1698 but did not like its position. It then belonged to "Mr Cotton JP". (3) In July 1774, Elizabeth, daughter of William Cotton, married Thomas Sheppard. He was created a baronet in 1809. He died in 1821 and was succeeded by his son Sir Thomas Cotton Sheppard who presumably rebuilt the house. (4) The house was occupied by Lady Sheppard in both 1834 and 1851. (5)

It was two-storey and rendered. Full details are available from the sale particulars of January 1900. It was let to Charles Tyrrell Cavendish on an annual tenancy at a rent of £450pa. The house was described as being built of brick with a stuccoed front and lead and slated roof, entered through a massive glazed portico into the entrance hall, a portion of which was fitted as a sitting room. Off the entrance hall were the dining and drawing rooms. Other reception rooms were the boudoir, study, the blue room and billiard room.

On the first floor were four main bedrooms, two with dressing rooms and eight other secondary bed and dressing rooms. On the second floor were four secondary bedrooms and four servants' rooms.

The "Domestic Offices" comprised, on the ground floor, the servants' hall, kitchen, two larders, dairy, scullery, lamp room, butler's pantry and bedroom, strong room, housekeeper's room and house maid's room. There were six cellars. The outbuildings included a bake house and brew house. A park of 41 acres included a couple of lakes, gardens, three vineries, peach house and much more. CT Cavendish, his wife and maid were on the *RMS Titanic.* The women survived the ordeal, but he went down with the ship.

Mrs Cavendish remained at the hall until her death in 1963, although the house was let out in apartments. Her son took up residence until 1968, when it was sold.

In 1972, the property was acquired by J.C. Bamford. It was gutted by fire in 1982 and the building was subsequently demolished. Houses have now been built on the site.

SUMMARY OF ACCOMMODATION.

ENTRANCE HALL AND SITTING ROOM.
DINING ROOM.
DRAWING ROOM.
BOUDOIR.
STUDY.
BLUE ROOM.
BILLIARD ROOM.

SIX PRINCIPAL BED AND DRESSING ROOMS.
TWELVE SECONDARY BED AND DRESSING ROOMS.
THREE WATER CLOSETS.
FOUR SERVANTS' BED ROOMS.
COMMODIOUS OFFICES.
EXTENSIVE CELLARAGE.

THE OUTBUILDINGS

Are conveniently situated near the Mansion, and consist of Wash House, two Store Houses, two Ash Bins, Laundry, Bake House, Brew House, three Servants' Closets and Urinal.

The Pleasure Grounds and Environment of the Residence

Are in a large measure of that interesting and historical character peculiar to the Ancestral Properties of England. At a slight remove from the Western side of the House is

A FINE OLD-WORLD FLOWER GARDEN AND ROSERY,

Approached by a winding path, sheltered by well-matured Yews and Ornamental Shrubs. A series of winding Wilderness Walks, screened by British Forest and Coniferous Trees, also lead to the large Southern Lake, which in turn is crossed by an artistic Foot Bridge.

On the North-West of the House is

A CREEPER-CLAD GARDENER'S COTTAGE,

Containing Living Room, Sitting Room, Wash House, Laundry, Cellar, three Bed Rooms and two Closets.

In the Frame Yard adjoining is a Cucumber House, Store House, lean-to Shed with Stoke Hole, lean-to Store Shed and Secondary Stoke Hole. There are also

A RANGE OF THREE VINERIES,

Another Range containing lean-to Double Conservatory, late Vinery with Peach House at end. There is

AN EXCELLENT WALLED-IN FRUIT AND VEGETABLE GARDEN

With a Range of brick and slated Sheds, comprising Coke Store, Potting Shed, Store House, Gardener's Office and Mushroom House at end, two Forcing Houses and two Frame Pits. There are

Part of the sale catalogue of 1900

Above: Crakemarsh in 1839. The left wing features in the photographs on p 64

Below: A later view of the house

Two views showing the wing of the house. The bottom view is the left side of the top one

Dilhorne Hall, Dilhorne

Demolished

Older halls called Dilhorne once stood on this site and a monument in Dilhorne Church has this inscription: " Here lieth the body of Copwood Hollins, late of Dilhorne Hall, who died August 25th 1705, aged 53 years." Copwood, who was the son of Philip Hollins, died without children and the hall became the property of Thomas Harrison. (1) Thomas Harrison married into the Holliday family.

The later hall was owned by John Holliday, who in 1790 had planted some hundred thousand trees around his manor and received an Arts and Manufacturers Society medal for doing so. He died in 1801, leaving the estate to his two-year-old grandson. His widow, together with his daughter, Mrs Buller, managed the estate until he came of age. (2) According to John Sneyd's diary, an entry in 1830 records him going to Dilhorne to see "Buller's new house". That it had been rebuilt is also recorded later as White's *Directory* of 1851 describes Dilhorne Hall as "Built about 20 years ago for Edward Buller Esq, Lord of the Manor, in the ancient style of brick and stone". Trubshaw of Great Haywood designed this new hall, where Edward Buller was still living in 1860, the year in which his wife Mary Ann died. (3)

In 1863 Edward Buller married Georgina Charlotte, his second wife, daughter and heiress of Sir Charles Edmund Nugent and widow of the Hon. George Banks MP. (4) Georgina Buller died in 1875. Edward and Georgina lived in London in 1871 with Georgina's son. They had no fewer than eleven servants to cater for their needs. Dilhorne Hall was occupied by Edward Buller's sons, Reginald, Frederick and Ernest in 1871.

In 1881 Edward Manningham Buller, baronet, was at Dilhorne Hall with his three sons, his daughter-in-law Mary and three grandchildren. No fewer than seventeen servants looked after these five adults and three children. Two of the servants were soldiers looking after their officers. Captain Reginald Manningham Buller served in the Grenadier Guards and his brother Captain Frederick Charles Manningham Buller in the Coldstream Guards. The domestic staff included a butler, cook, lady's maid, housemaids, laundry maids, kitchen and scullery maids, footmen and a groom.

The Buller family left Dilhorne in 1924 and the property was advertised for sale in 1927. After the hall was demolished in 1959 some of the stone was used for local roads. The crown bowling green at Dilhorne recreation centre is on the site of the hall.

Dilhorne Hall and its park. Note the windmill on the left and the church to the right. The house portrayed was replaced by the house shown below

Etruria Hall, Etruria
Hotel

This red brick hall was built in 1769 as a home for Josiah Wedgwood. It was designed by Joseph Pickford of Derby. Originally it was a square, three-storey house with stone dressings. It had five bays at the front with three, slightly projecting, central bays surmounted by a pediment. There were vaulted cellars below where Wedgwood had a private laboratory where he experimented to improve his ceramic bodies, colours and glazes. Wedgwood extended the hall, in 1780, to accommodate his growing family. Two flanking wings were added in the 19th century but were demolished a few years ago as part of a restoration scheme, returning the property to its 18th century appearance. The household staff, in 1794, comprised seven male servants including a butler and gardener, a housekeeper and many female servants. The family had ten horses and six carriages. After Josiah's death in 1795 the family continued to live at the hall but the building was later used as a boarding school before again becoming a home for Francis Wedgwood, younger son of Josiah II. Later the hall was sold to the Duchy of Lancaster and let to various tenants including Earl Granville who established a new branch of the Shelton Ironworks on a site to the west of the hall.

From 1892 the hall was used as offices for the Shelton Iron, Steel and Coal Co. Ltd who bought it from the Duchy in 1930. For decades the former house existed in the middle of heavy industry. Used as the headquarters of the National Garden Festival in 1986, it became the property of Stoke-on-Trent City Council, who leased it to St. Modwen Properties who were joint developers of the former Shelton Bar site, now Festival Park.

The hall and surrounding land were sublet by St. Modwen's to Queens Moat Houses for the building of a hotel complex. This new complex cost £16 million. (1)

Etruria Hall. Within a century or so, this house was to find itself situated in an area of heavy industry (iron and steel in particular)

Fenton Hall, Fenton

Demolished

This sketch shows a large, two-storeyed, Georgian house with a porch and pediment above, known as Fenton Hall. Routes of two proposed railways can be seen and the hall was demolished in 1847 when the railways were being constructed. The latter were for the Manchester and Tamworth Railway and the Manchester, Cheshire and Staffordshire Railway and both were on 35 feet high embankments. Fenton Hall was owned in the 1730s by William Cotton of Crakemarsh. He was followed by John Peate, who became bankrupt. In 1748 Thomas Whieldon, a potter, purchased the hall and the adjoining potworks from the bankrupt Peate. In 1797 Josiah Spode II returned from London to live at Fenton Hall following the death of his father. Members of the Adams family of potters later occupied the hall. Mrs Sarah Adams is listed in White's *Directory* of 1834 as the occupier of it. On the illustration of Fenton Hall is another large house known simply as Fenton. The illustrations were part of a petition to Parliament against the two railway lines.

Top: Fenton

Right: Fenton Hall with two railway lines cutting through its site (from left to right)
The nearest of the two railway lines was that of the Manchester and Tamworth Railway

The Field, High Street, Leek

National Reserve Club

William Philips, who was a lieutenant in the Leek Volunteer Corps, built this house, also known as Field House, around 1804. It is rumoured that he stopped the builders several times, fearing a French invasion, as he said that "he wouldn't build quarters for Boney's soldiers". Samuel Philips and his brother William lived here in 1818. (1) They were silk manufacturers whose factory was in Barngates (now West Street). Samuel died in 1851 and William in 1871 when the house passed to Thomas Whittles. The Whittles family occupied the house for over 30 years. In 1891, Catherine Whittles, Thomas' widow, is described as a sewing silk manufacturer, employing 71 full-time and 14 half-time hands. The Whittles' silk mill was Wellington Mill on Strangman Street. The family was able to walk from their home to their factory without encountering any other houses.

In the early 1900s, the estate was purchased by the town. In 1904 new streets (High Street, Field Street and Salisbury Street) were laid out on the estate and shops and commercial premises were built; with Field House facing the new High Street. In 1905 the town still owned an unsold portion of the Fields estate adjoining these new streets. At the time of the sale, Field House had three reception rooms, a kitchen and three good cellars. Upstairs were seven bedrooms and a box room. Dr F.E. Fieldon practised from Field House in 1908 and a commercial hotel offered tea, bed and breakfast for 4/6d in 1912. The house was used as a registration centre for those enlisting in World War I and later became Leek National Reserve Club, fondly known as "The Nash".

The Field before the breakup of the estate

The Firs, Newcastle-under-Lyme
Museum and Art Gallery

This large house is situated on The Brampton in Newcastle. It was built for Thomas Leech and designed by the architect Charles Lynam. The house had been completed in 1855 and the date of construction is commemorated by the date stone above the original entrance. It is an attractive building of red brick with stone dressings and Lynam ornamented the main façade with various architectural features including a stone balcony under the window on the first floor. The house was offered to let in the *Staffordshire Advertiser* on 4th August 1855, describing it as having dining, drawing and breakfast rooms, of spacious dimensions, together with good kitchens, on the ground floor. There were six bedrooms on the first floor, and one on the second. Outside was a stable and coach house.

It was let to various tenants over the years until Leech sold the house to Ralph Moseley, in 1863, for £3,400. The Firs was home to the Moseley family, who were drapers in Newcastle, until Ralph died in 1914. William Simmons bought the house that same year, later selling it to Harry Scrivener Adams in 1922. Adams enlarged the house with various extensions. The executors of Harry S. Evans sold it to Newcastle Borough Council in 1956 for £6,325.They opened it as a museum and art gallery shortly afterwards.

The house today, now Newcastle's Museum and Art Gallery

Ford Green Hall, Smallthorne, Stoke-on-Trent

Museum

In 1974, Pevsner described Ford Green Hall as a lovely, timber-framed house with a two-bay Georgian addition. William Ford had built a house at Ford Green in c. 1580, which later became known as Ford Green Hall. The builder was thought to be Raphe Sutton whose inscription can be seen over a doorway in the hall. The two-storeyed entrance porch at the front was probably added about 1620. The original wattle and daub infill would have been covered with plaster and then painted, but later the outside of the house was covered with a stucco of lath and plaster. An inventory dated 1713 reveals the layout of the house. On the ground floor were the house place, the central hall, the little kitchen, the parlour and the near and far butteries. Upstairs were the buttery chamber, the house chamber, the parlour chamber and the porch chamber. Outside there was also a chamber over the stable and two cocklofts. There is evidence in the roof timbers that an original east timber-framed wing was replaced by brick in c. 1734. The Ford family continued to live at Ford Green Hall through several generations. The last family to live there were Hugh Ford and his wife Mary who died in 1782 and 1785 respectively. They left four daughters and after the youngest daughter, Catherine, came of age in 1803, the property was sold. (1) The Warburton family, who were potters, owned the house in the early 19th century. (2) In 1946 the dilapidated house was bought by the city of Stoke-on-Trent for £1,100. The timber exterior still covered in stucco was damaged by flood water from a nearby stream. The stream was culverted at a cost of £18,000 and a further £9,000 was spent on restoring the hall. It was opened as a folk museum in 1952 and is still open to the public.

Above: The front of the house today Opposite page: The rear of the house

Foxlowe, Market Place, Leek

Licensed Premises

This house, at the top of the Market Place, was the home of the Mills family during the latter half of the 18th century and early 19th century. They were prominent lawyers in the town. Many local history books relate that when Bonnie Prince Charlie came to Leek in 1745, he stayed at the home of William Mills at the top of the Market Place. It has always been assumed that it was this house, which later became known as Foxlowe. A document reveals that, in fact, William Mills had two smaller houses here in 1745. They were pulled down after this date and this larger house built on the same site.

In 1819 Thomas Mills sold the house to John Cruso snr, who was also a lawyer. He died in 1841 and the house, known then as no.1 Market Place, passed to his son John jnr. The latter was first married to Mary Badnall. After Mary died he occupied this huge house by himself apart from his servants. The 1851 census of Leek reveals that John Cruso, a widower and magistrate, aged 61, lived here with his housekeeper, cook, kitchen maid, housemaid, laundress and footman. He also employed a coachman who lived round the corner in Cruso's Yard. In 1851 John Cruso was also the Manor Steward of Leek. He then married Ann Searight and it is this second wife who became well known for her charitable deeds and good works. When John Cruso died in 1867 his will refers to the house on the north side of the Market Place, Leek, with gardens, pleasure grounds, servants' cottages and coach houses. The land consisted of the field below the garden and churchyard and the fishpond plus a field to the north of the fishpond, which was used as a kitchen garden. Mrs Cruso was still living at this house in 1892, but it was up for sale in 1893. In 1901 it was the home of Mary J. Gailey, a widow, and her son Josiah Brunt. George Davenport bought the house and gave it the name of Foxlowe, presumably after the area of land in the valley beyond the house. In 1914 the house was advertised for sale in the local paper. It was described as a Georgian house with gardens, grounds, three acres of land and three closes of excellent grassland of fifteen and a half acres. It had four reception rooms, a billiard room, 13 bed and dressing rooms and was fitted with electric lights and heated.

Outside was a coachman's house, stabling for five horses, a garage for two cars, a coach house and two excellent tennis courts formed of brick ash. The land stretched down to the bottom of what is now Brough Park situated behind this property. In living memory there was a pond at the bottom of the park, that used to be Mrs Cruso's fishpond.

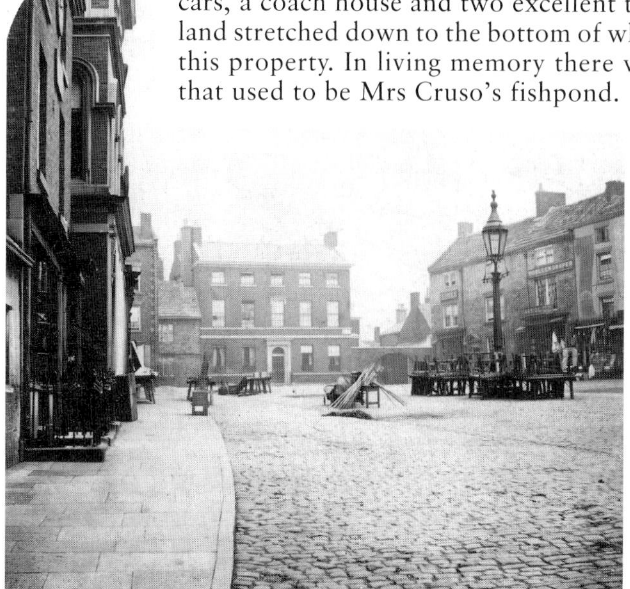

On this occasion the house failed to reach its reserve price and so remained the property of Mrs Davenport, who allowed it to be used as a convalescent home for wounded soldiers during the Great War. In 1919 seven local trade unions came together to form the Amalgamated Society of Textile and Kindred Trades (1) and Foxlowe became their headquarters. *Kelly's Directory* of 1932 lists the Foxlowe Trade and Labour Club at this address. After the union left, the building was empty and neglected for a number of years. It is now the V-Bar.

Above & opposite: Two views of Foxlowe from the Market Place, Leek. The Parker House (see p.117) adjoins it

Greenhill House, Cheadle

Demolished

The house was built c. 1710 by Mr Leigh, who died in 1767 leaving it to his wife and children. In 1767 a marriage settlement describes this as "a new erected capital; messuage or tenement". It was then the property of Mr Edward Leigh. (1) The house was sold, in 1806, to Thomas Griffin whose two unmarried daughters lived there for the rest of their lives. They are listed as residents in *White's Directory* of 1834. The last of the Griffin sisters died in 1849 and the house sold to Mr Paddock. He built the southwest wing and then let the property as two residences. The tenants in 1860 were John Bates and William Nutt. (2) The house was sold to Mr C. J. Blagg in 1867. (3) In 1869 further additions were made to the house on the north side and the property was modernised and reconverted to one house. Plant, in 1881, described it as one of the finest residences near Cheadle. It was the home, at that time of Charles Blagg, a local solicitor, his wife and their 8 children. His elder son was an undergraduate at Oxford University while the youngest child was aged only three. This large household had a staff of upper and under housemaids, upper and under nurses, a cook, a kitchen maid and a groom. Greenhill House was demolished in 1930.

Greenway Bank, Norton-in-the-Moors
Demolished

Greenway Bank was the property of Hugh Henshall, the brother of Ann Henshall who married James Brindley, the noted canal engineer. Henshall purchased the property in c. 1778. When Hugh died in 1817 he left this property to his niece, Ann Brindley, the eldest daughter of James. If Ann were to marry, or on the event of her death, Greenway Bank was to pass to her half-brother Hugh Henshall Williamson. (1) Hugh Williamson rebuilt the house in 1828. (2)

He was already living at Greenway Bank in 1834, before Ann Brindley died at sea in 1838. At this time Hugh was High Sheriff of Staffordshire. (3) Census returns and directories reveal that Hugh and his family lived at Greenway Bank for many years.

The house was offered for sale in 1871 and the auction advertisement described Greenway Bank as "a freehold property, situated in Norton-in-the-Moors, with the minerals thereunder, comprising a spacious manor house and pleasure grounds, entrance hall, dining room, drawing room, breakfast and other sitting rooms, butlers pantry and plate closet, housekeepers room and servants hall, extensive sleeping accommodation, dressing rooms, closets, domestic offices fitted with every modern convenience." The sale also included excellent stabling, loose box, harness room, coach house, shrubberies, fish ponds, walled and other gardens, orchards, vineries, conservatories, greenhouse and extensive walks laid out through plantations and woodlands adjacent to a large sheet of ornamental water.

The auction took place at the Railway Hotel, Stoke (4) when Mr Robert Heath purchased Greenway Bank with its pleasure grounds and 214 acres for £19,000 with a payment of £1,385 for growing timber. In 1872 Robert Heath bought Biddulph Grange and left his son, also Robert, living at Greenway Bank with his wife Laura and their five children. (5) In 1881 Robert Heath, described as an ironmaster, was living at Greenway Bank with his wife and 4 young children. The youngest child was a baby only 4 months old, explaining the need to employ a monthly nurse, a head nurse and under nurse, as well as a cook, housemaid and a kitchen maid. Robert lived at Greenway Bank until 1901 when he moved to Biddulph Grange. Members of the Heath family lived here until 1971.

Staffordshire County Council bought the land from the estates of Greenway Bank and Knypersley Hall (a mile to the north) in 1973. Greenway Bank House was said to be badly decayed and was demolished, but some of the old outbuildings were renovated and now form an estate yard and visitor centre. The main car park is in the old kitchen gardens; some of the original fruit trees can still be seen around the walls. An old croquet lawn and tennis court have been used for the overflow car park. Today, Greenway Bank is a country park enjoyed by the people of nearby Stoke-on- Trent. It stretches down to Knypersley Reservoir, built by the Trent & Mersey Canal Co., in which Hugh Henshall was a shareholder and partner.

Opposite top: Greenway Bank, c.1840, the seat of H.H. Williamson

Opposite bottom: The house just prior to demolition

Hales Hall, Oakamoor Road, Cheadle

Cheadle Camping and Caravan Park

This lovely house stood in parkland and was built of brick with stone facings and corner pilasters. It was built in 1712 in Queen Anne style by Archibald Grosvenor for himself and his wife, Frances. She was the granddaughter of Sir Matthew Hale, hence the name of the house. Hale was Lord Chief Justice of England in the reign of Charles II. (1) Archibald Grosvenor died in 1725 and his wife Frances in 1727 (2). There is a tomb and various monuments to the Grosvenor family in Cheadle Parish Church. In the 1820s, Hales Hall was the home of Isabella Bacon, a close friend of Penelope Sneyd, and in 1828, Baddeley Child lived there. In his will dated 1830, Edward Smith Grosvenor, formerly of Hales Hall, left money for the poor of Cheadle. (3)

The Rev. Edward Whieldon, vicar of Bradley-in-the-Moors, purchased the property in 1841 (4). He was succeeded by his son, also Edward. Reverend Edward Whieldon, the vicar of Bradley and Croxton, lived here in 1881 with his wife and two of his nieces. The Whieldons employed a cook, a parlour maid, a housemaid and a page. In addition to his clerical duties the vicar was also farming 47 acres of land. Edward was descended from Thomas Whieldon, the potter, of Fenton Hall.

Robert Heywood was the tenant of Hales Hall when it was advertised for sale in 1919 by order of Lieut-Colonel Eardley-Wilmot C.M.G. The sale catalogue describes the Hall as "occupying a delightful, sheltered position about 550ft above sea level, overlooking well wooded scenery and surrounded by charming pleasure grounds, gardens and well timbered pasture land of over 26 acres". Purchasers of the hall would also have sole right of fishing, boating and grazing over the lake and its banks. The house had a spacious entrance hall, dining room, drawing room, library and an anteroom. Several of these rooms had oak wainscoting. In addition to the usual kitchen, scullery and larder was a butler's pantry. On the first floor were six bedrooms and dressing rooms and a bathroom. Six additional bedrooms were located on the second floor. The mansion was lit by acetylene gas and mains water was laid on.

The outbuildings comprised stables for five horses, a harness room, two large coach or motor houses with lofts over, a man's living rooms, dairy, pigeon and fowl houses and a gas house. The spacious grounds had lawns, flower gardens, two tennis lawns and shrubberies. A conservatory adjoined the dining room and the walled kitchen garden boasted two vineries.

The house was purchased in c. 1945 by Thomas Bolton & Sons Ltd who divided it and let it to various members of their senior staff. One of the tenants was Dr. W.E. Alkins, a former director of the company, whose interest in daffodil species may be seen each spring.

The elegant Queen Anne front of the original house

The house with an extension to the left, later extended (below)

Haregate Hall, Haregate Road, Leek

Three dwellings

Sleigh, in his *History of the Ancient Parish of Leek*, describes Haregate as a quaint 17th century English gentleman's house with Dutch-like fish ponds and pleasaunce (sic). The main range of the house does date from the 17th century or earlier and is built of ashlar stone and consists of one storey with attics. A "parlour block" of red brick was added at the east end in the 18th century. This addition is of two storeys with attics and the VCH stables incorrectly that it was remodelled in the 19th century, retaining some of the original interiors. (1)

The house passed to Sir Ralph Bagnall in 1552. (2) After being bought and sold many times over the ensuing years, Joshua Toft, a Quaker button merchant, bought Haregate in 1720 and was still living there in 1745, when Bonnie Prince Charlie and his Highland army came through the town. The Highlanders had to leave their arms at Haregate's front door before being fed with boiled beef and vegetables. (3)

Ann FormW the widow of Josiah Ford, married Joshua Toft and took her two young children to live at Haregate. Her husband, also a Quaker, had been a great friend of Joshua Toft. The latter died in 1769 and his daughter, Mary, from his first marriage inherited Haregate. She was by then the widow of Charles Chorley. (4) White's *Directory* of 1851 lists Edward Chorley, Esq as having a seat in Tittesworth called Haregate. Edward was Charles and Mary Chorle{\ö grandson.

The estate passed from the Chorleys to Elizabeth Atkinson, née Chorley, and then to her daughter Susannah, wife of Frank Atkinson Argles. Frank Argles lived at the hall from time to time but it was also let out to tenants incl z ng W illiam Edward Challinor and Ernest Worthington. Frank Argles' son, Thomas, was living at Haregate by 1900. Thomas Argles died in 1923 and the hall became the property of his first cousin, R.M. Argles. Mr Argles employed a gamekeeper to rear the pheasants and to arrange the shoots attended by many of Leek's mill owners. (5) Leek Urban District Council bought the hall and 78 e 6es of land in 1948 for £13,500. They converted the house to three dwellings and laid out the council estate of 268 houses on the land. (6) Haregate Road and Argles Road derive their names from the former hall and one of the former owners.

Opposite page: Views of the two wings of Haregate Hall, taken when the house was a country seat

Harewood Hall, Leek Road, Cheadle
Mental Care Home

The hall was built in Harwood Lane, now Leek Road, and to improve the sound of the name an "e" was inserted, and the house became known as Harewood Park. (1) It was built in 1860 in brick for William Bowers, who died in 1880. His son, William Eli, who was born there in 1861, inherited the hall. In 1881, William's widow, Hannah, was at Harewood with her son William who was an undergraduate. Their household staff comprised a cook, housemaid, kitchen maid and a page. William Eli fenced the property, putting up iron rails along Harwood Lane and Bate Lane. (2) He died in 1911 at Caverswall Castle.

A sale catalogue dated 1918 described the house as having a lounge entrance with a Minton tiled floor, a small office, a dining room with large bay and a conservatory adjoining. The drawing room had three bays and a handsome cut glass chandelier and side gas brackets. There was also a garden entrance. The first floor had nine bedrooms and dressing rooms, a bathroom and sewing room. On the second floor were three maids' bedrooms and another bedroom. The house had cellars as well as the usual kitchens, pantry, laundry room and linen and drying rooms. Outside were pleasure grounds including a croquet lawn, a tennis lawn and a pitch pine summer house. There were two walled kitchen gardens and fruit trees. The greenhouse had two plant houses and two vineries. The stabling was built in brick and located round an enclosed yard. It comprised two loose boxes, a four-stall stable with lofts and grooms' room, a saddle room, two coach houses and a coalhouse. The grounds extended to nearly 40 acres.

The house in 1906

Highfield Hall, Macclesfield Road, Leek

Demolished

Richard Badnall built the house, it was in c. 1819 on land purchased by his father, Joseph, in 1801. Richard, a silk dyer in Leek, went bankrupt in 1827 and the house was offered for sale at the Roebuck Hotel in Leek on 2nd August of that year.

The sales brochure describes Highfield House as a "spacious family residence with coach house, stables, outbuildings, lawn, garden, shrubberies, pleasure ground and several enclosures of meadow and arable land". The ground floor of the house had a handsome entrance hall, a paved inner hall and a stone staircase with iron balustrades, mahogany handrail and a dome light. On this floor were a library, breakfast parlour, gentleman's dressing room and an elegant bow-windowed drawing room richly papered and ornamented with gilt mouldings. The dining room had a marble chimney piece and mahogany panelled doors. Also on this floor were a china closet, butler's pantry, a lofty, light kitchen, a larder, scullery and laundry.

The first storey had five principal bedrooms, four dressing rooms, a large day nursery with washing room adjoining, two sleeping nurseries with children's dressing room, a WC and a housemaid's closet.

The upper storey had three servants' rooms and the basement had an arched wine vault, cellary (sic) and a cool dairy. Outside was a large paved yard, water well with lifting pump and apparatus, a knife house, brewhouse, ash hole, coal house and dung pit.

The stable block comprised a three-stall stable, coach house, harness room, a second three-stall stable with a granary and pigeon house over surmounted by a cupola and vane. The brochure also details a paved farm yard, cow house, wagon lodge, calf pen, thrashing barn, poultry house, piggeries and potato store. The grounds included a garden, lawn and pleasure ground and had a fish pond and a walled garden abundantly stocked and planted with fruit trees (which may be seen on the photograph on p.88).

In December of that year (1827) the house, together with 46 acres, was sold to Sarah Fowler and her sons, Matthew and Josiah Gaunt. The Gaunts were members of a Leek banking family. Charles Glover bought the house and 72 acres of land in 1870 and in 1885, Edwin Cliffe Glover sold it to Arthur Nicholson, son of Joshua Nicholson from the firm of Brough, Nicholson and Hall, textile manufacturers of Leek. Arthur added another wing to the house in 1889. He also built a stud farm north of the house and became a very successful breeder of shire horses. Arthur Nicholson was knighted in 1909 and in 1911 King George V and Queen Mary visited Highfield and were shown the horses. After Sir Arthur Nicholson died in 1929, his widow Marianne continued to live there. She died in 1937 and the house was sold in 1939 and demolished c. 1940. Surviving outbuildings include the present Home Farm, lodge and the former stable block also converted to a house. (1)

The Leek Town Football Club played on a pitch in the grounds of Highfield Hall by 1892 and early cricket clubs also played there. Leek Cricket Club now has its headquarters and pitch on the former front lawn.

Two views of the entrance front

Above: An evocative portrait of the entrance front

Below: Another view from the ha-ha of the entrance front. This also shows the alteration to the right hand side (compare with pp84 & 88)

LEEK : Staffordshire.

Adjoining the Town of Leek.

The Valuable and Attractive Freehold Residential and Agricultural : ESTATE. :

KNOWN AS

Highfield Hall Estate.

COMPRISING:

The Imposing Mansion : HIGHFIELD HALL.

Two Excellent Dairy Farms.

Five Choice Small Residences and Country Cottages.

The Home Farm and Stud Farm Buildings and Sound Lands.

Numerous Accommodation Fields.

To be SOLD BY AUCTION by

Messrs. W. S. BAGSHAW & SONS

at the RED LION HOTEL,

: LEEK, :

on MONDAY, the 15th MAY, 1939

at 2.30 o'clock in the Afternoon precisely, either as a whole or in numerous Lots (unless Sold in the meantime by Private Treaty), and subject to Conditions of Sale.

For Particulars, Plans and Conditions of Sale, apply to:—

Messrs. W. S. BAGSHAW & SONS, Auctioneers : Uttoxeter and Ashbourne.

Messrs. W. ELLAWAY SMITH & Co., Estate Agents : 6, Derby Street, Leek.

or to Messrs. CHALLINORS & SHAW, Solicitors : LEEK.

This page and opposite: Sale particulars of May 1939

LOT 1.

(WITH VACANT POSSESSION.)

The Charming Country Residence,

known as

" Highfield Hall,"

situate adjacent to the town of Leek, approached from the road leading from Leek to Macclesfield, and comprising :

THE MANSION,

a fine erection, substantially built of red brick with stone facings and leaded light windows, with slated and lead roof surmounted by a handsome weathervane, stands in attractive Grounds about 580 feet above sea level, with a pleasant south-west aspect ; is approached from the main road by a carriage drive lined with Rhododendrons, Shrubs and Forest Trees, and terminating in a gravelled forecourt.

The accommodation includes :

Portico, supported on 2 circular stone pillars.

A panelled oak door with leaded lights opens into **Small Vestibule** and

Lounge and **Staircase Hall,** with oak panelled dado and parquetry floor, fireplace in Inglenook with oak mantel.

Dining Room, 33′ × 17′, with handsome carved oak overmantel.

Drawing Room, 34′ 6″ × 16′, with large bay in addition, and carved mahogany mantel,

A pair of half-glazed oak doors lead into

The Conservatory, 76′ × 21′, and **Sun Loggia.**

Cloak Room, Lavatory and W.C.

The Oak Room or **Billiards Room,** about 36′ × 35′, having large bay with leaded windows, oak panelled round and oak floor ; Inglenook with carved oak mantel with fitted 8-day bracket clock.

A Side Entrance Portico with oak pillars leads to **Business Room,** 16′ × 16′, having oak floor and mahogany mantel, with 2 panels inlaid with ivory carvings.

THE DOMESTIC OFFICES

include Front Kitchen with Herald range ; Back Kitchen with fitted dresser ; 2 Pantries ; larder with white glazed walls and slate thrawling ; Servants' Hall, Store Room with cupboards and sink ; Butler's Pantry with 2 wood bowls (h. & c.) and draining boards, fitted cupboards round ; a safe door by Thomas Skidmore.

Side Entrance with cloak room, wash basins and W.C.

Extensive Cellarage.

—3—

Above: A lovely view of the rear of the house and conservatory

Below: An early aerial view of the house, outbuildings and the kitchen garden taken prior to the redevelopment of the conservatory wing

Horton Lodge, Rudyard

Community Special School

Stephen Chesters-Thompson, of the Manchester-based Chesters brewing family, built Horton Lodge in 1890. He was one of the investors in Clough Hall Park and Garden (see p.53). Horton Lodge was offered for sale in 1894 but failed to reach the reserve price of £6,000. William Anthony Marsden Tellwright, owner of the Sneyd Collieries, finally purchased it later that year. William Tellwright paid £5,750, which fell far short of Chesters-Thompson's original outlay of £14,000. He must have extended it for the tower is dated 1909. Horton Lodge became the North Staffordshire Collieries Owners Association Convalescent Home from 1925 to 1948. (1) Horton Lodge was then used for weekend courses by the WEA. (2) Stoke-on-Trent Education Committee bought the property in 1950 for use as a special school and it is still a community special school.

Huntley Hall, Mobberley, Cheadle

Demolished

The hall, with its two lodges, stood south-west of Cheadle and was backed by a sandstone hill. It was built in 1829 for Captain Clement Sneyd, RN, who was born in 1773. This handsome residence had five principal rooms on the ground floor and eight bedrooms on the first floor. Outside were a small stable block and a coach house. (1) The 1841 census lists Captain Sneyd, with his daughters Rosamund and Caroline, in residence at the hall. Clement Sneyd was promoted to Rear Admiral in 1846. After his death, in 1854, the hall passed to his daughter Caroline who had married Reverend George Mather. The Mathers were living at the hall by 1860, the year Caroline died. By 1871 George was obviously augmenting his income by taking in private pupils. Two of the pupils were Clement Sneyd Kinnersley and his brother John. In 1881 George Mather was resident at the hall with his son and four daughters. He still had two private pupils who were also resident at the hall. After George's death his son, Frederic occupied Huntley. A sale notice of March 1927 describes the hall as a country residence having lounge, dining and drawing rooms, smoking room, butler's pantry, maid's sitting room, kitchen, larder and boot room on the ground floor, eight bedrooms and dressing rooms on the first floor and servants' accommodation on the second floor. Outside were stabling and outbuildings, the whole surrounded by 15 acres of land.

The stable block survives, but most of the house was demolished in the late 1920s.

Ilam Hall, Ilam

Mostly demolished

The Port family were possibly established at Ilam shortly after November 1547, when they purchased ex-Burton-on-Trent Abbey lands from William Paget. (1) Their house appears to have been fairly plain with unusual chimneys. It was bought by Jesse Watts Russell's father in 1770. (2) It was replaced in 1821 by a new house built by Jesse Watts Russell in Gothic Revival style. The construction appears to have started just about the time Alton Abbey was finished (see p.14) and may have been influenced by the Earl of Shrewsbury's home. Certainly Watts Russell became well known for his interest in this style of architecture. In 1819, he built a chapel on the north side of the church in the same style, both being designed by John Shaw. The contractor was James Trubshaw of Great Haywood, Staffordshire. Work on the house started on 29th January 1821, the anniversary of Watts Russell's wedding day and the birth of his father-in-law, David Pike Watts, who is commemorated by the carving in the north chapel in Ilam Church. It was finished in September 1826. (3)

Following the death of Jesse Watts Russell, the estate, extending to 998 acres, was put up for auction in 1875. Starting at £50,000 it was runup to £73,000 when it was withdrawn. It was then purchased by the Rt. Hon. Robert W. Hanbury MP, later President of the Board of Agriculture. This was the position he held in the Government at the time of his death in May 1903, leaving £104,667. A dispute on his will went to the House of Lords where his nieces succeeded in a ruling that Mrs Hanbury only had a life interest in the Hall (in February 1905). A year later, her jewellery, worth several thousand pounds, was stolen at Euston railway station. Described as "The Hanbury Jewels", was this theft or pre-arranged? Mrs Hanbury remarried in 1904 to a Mr Bowring who added Hanbury to his surname. They took up residence at Ilam in June 1904, just over a year after Robert Hanbury's death.

In July 1910, the estate, consisting of the hall and 852 acres, was offered for sale again. It had a reserve of £54,000 and was withdrawn at £38,500. It appears to have been sold privately and opened as a hotel. By the early 1930s, it was empty and deteriorating. A youth hostel for 32 people opened in 1932, probably in buildings at the rear. Whether this remained open is unclear, but the current youth hostel opened in 1935 following demolition of the formal rooms.

The building was built of gritstone from nearby Stanton (to the west). The presence of barytes in the matrix gave the stone a peach-coloured appearance. It must have looked rather well when initially constructed. A house on the Derby road at Cromford was built with materials from the Hall. These include a marble fireplace, oak doors and what appear to be Minton floor tiles from the conservatory. Some of the stone retains its "peach" colour.

Left: The Ports' house, replaced in 1821 by J. Watts Russell

Below: In Gothic Revival style, this house survived until 1935

Above: The Billiard Room. The fireplace on the right was purchased from the demolition contractors by Elstree Studios. It was descibed as being Jacobean

Right: The Drawing Room which looked out towards the church. It was at first floor level on the view on p.94 (bottom)

Above: At the rear, adjoining the Italianate Garden was the Orangery. Portrayed are Mr Hanbury with his wife and mother

Left: The Inner Hall. This is part of the Common Room of the Youth Hostel, saved from demolition by a donation of £500 from John Cadbury, the chocolate maker and YHA Chairman, at the behest of his wife. The screen was lost, however. From the room beyond, two doors on the left gave access to the principal rooms of the house

Above: The Music Room Below: The Library

KEELE HALL, KEELE

UNIVERSITY

The Sneyds had owned Keele Manor for many years before building a house there, having made their money in business at Chester and in shrewd land purchases in North Staffordshire, from where they emanated.

The first house on the site was built in 1580 (1) but it was 1757 before further work was done on the house when the east end was rebuilt. At the same time the kitchen garden was laid out, together with the surrounding wall and a dovecote. The garden was in use from 1764. Landscaping and extension of the park seems to have been the major preoccupation for nearly 100 years. Initially William Emes was employed. He had been the head gardener at Kedleston, Derbyshire, between 1756 and 1760 and was then well established as a landscape gardener/architect. (2) This work included the millpond of the former Keele Forge, which Goodway believes is one of the earliest examples in the country of the deliberate reclamation of a disused industrial site. (3)

Between 1833 and 1834, new stables (now The Clock House) were built by Edward Blore on the site of an earlier block and the adjacent farm buildings demolished (replaced by the Home Farm). In 1855 work commenced on the demolition of the old house and Anthony Salvin was appointed architect to build a larger but similar Jacobean-style house to the earlier one. This was very much in keeping with Ralph Sneyd's conservative tastes. (4)

By 1872-73, the estate extended to 9,232 acres. (5) Ralph Sneyd employed 21 servants at Keele in 1891. In 1901 the hall was let to the Grand Duke Michael of Russia who entertained King Edward VII there. The Grand Duke, who had made a morganatic marriage with Countess Sophie of Merenberg, stayed at Keele for ten years.

Requisitioned by the Army during World War II, the hall was left in the usual ex-Army state of worse than found. In 1949, the excess of nearly 100 army huts found a new use as the University College of North Staffordshire when the hall and 150 acres were purchased. It is now the University of Keele.

As work must have been reaching its conclusion at Keele, a fire destroyed the central part of Capesthorne Hall, home of the Bromley – Davenports who also owned Wootton Hall. Salvin was called in to rebuild the gutted area of this house, situated south-west of Macclesfield in Cheshire.

Above: Keele in 1686 from Plot's History of Staffordshire

Below: Salvin's self-assured Jacobean-style house of 1856

Knypersley Hall, Knypersley

Reduced

The old hall was built in Henry II's reign and was the seat of the Knypersley branch of the Biddulph family. It passed to the Bowyers by marriage and became the seat of Sir William Bowyer before passing to the Gresley family. An inventory dating from 1701 describes the layout of the house. A kitchen, hall, parlour, pantry and cellar were mentioned. On the first floor was a chamber over the parlour, a middle chamber, a hall chamber and a chamber over the kitchen. There was also a brew house and a cockloft with bedrooms over. (1) Sir Nigel Gresley, Bt, modernised this ancient mansion with a brick casing about 1760. However the drawing opposite shows this house ruined in 1836 and it is built of stone.

James Bateman of Salford bought it for £37,000 in 1809 from the executors of Sir Nigel Gresley. He bought it for his son, John Bateman, on the occasion of his marriage to Elizabeth Holt of Redivals. James Bateman, John's son, lived here before moving to Biddulph Grange circa 1842. John Bateman and his wife, Elizabeth, were resident at Knypersley in 1841. He described himself as a landed proprietor and employed a butler, footman, housekeeper, lady's maid, kitchen maid, under housemaid and a housemaid. The *Staffordshire Advertiser* described the accommodation at Knypersley in 1853 as being "plain, unostentatious, substantial and replete, with every accessory and convenience which elegance and refined taste could devise". In 1858 the third floor of the house was removed and the size much reduced. (2)

The house, reduced in size was offered for sale in 1996 as a Grade II listed building. The sale description includes a lounge with an original Rococo plaster ceiling. This had arabesques interfaced with cartouches, shells, ribands, baskets of flowers, branches of blossoms and delicate sheaves, all in deep relief with special attention drawn to the elaborate centrepiece. The asking price was £550,000.

Knypersley New Hall in 1847

Remains of the Old Hall, Knypersley, in 1836

Leek, The Hall House, Market Place

Public House.

The Red Lion in Leek Market Place was once the town house of Thomas Jolliffe, a wealthy mercer. It was built in 1627 and was probably the largest timber framed building in the town. (1) Next door was a smaller and earlier house, also owned by the Jolliffe's, which was pulled down to make way for the Market hall in 1897. This smaller house contained an ornamented plaster ceiling, demonstrating the wealth and status of the family. The ceiling was saved when the house was demolished. The Hall House had three storeys, an attic and a cellar and was built with a double pile plan. This was an English seventeenth century house plan consisting of a rectangular block two rooms deep, the rooms sometimes separated by a passage. A Thomas Jolliffe, who died in 1758, was the last member of the family to own this house, which was sold as part of the Jolliffe estates in 1765. The precise date when the property became an inn is not known. However, the house was refronted and a large extension added, in 1791, providing extra accommodation and stabling for eight horses. Initials of MD on a rainwater head suggest that Michael Daintry had this extension built. He was certainly the owner in 1808 when the innkeeper was Michael Stubbs. (2)

Above & opposite: The right-hand three-storey building is the Red Lion Inn in the Market Place, Leek. Formerly the Hall House, it was refronted and extended c. 1791. The adjacent two-storey building was older and its loss to the town was significant, although perhaps not appreciated at the time

Two panels from the ornamented plaster ceiling of the building adjacent to the Hall House

Lightoaks, Cheadle Road, Oakamoor

House extended, c. 1890

In 1986 the house was described as of mid-19th century date in roughcast brick with slate roof and roughcast stacks. It had an irregular plan with the principal entrance to the north and garden fronts to the east and south with a service yard to the west. A covered arcade led to the greenhouse. The north front was of two storeys and had attics and cellars. Three gabled bays are described, each gable having shaped bargeboards and casements with patterned glazing bars; also a central *porte-cochere* of two open, arched bays. The south front had three gabled bays with shaped bargeboards and casements with patterned glazing bars, those to the ground floor left and right were barge windows with hipped roofs. (1) Lightoaks was built in the 1820s for John Wilson Patten who was MP for South Lancashire. He married Miss Hyde from Wootton Lodge and was later Baron Winmarleigh. The Patten family of Warrington established the Cheadle Copper and Brass works in 1734. They lived at Lightoaks in 1828 (2) and were probably still there until the house was rented to Captain John Ireland Blackbourne, a county magistarate.(3)

The house was offered for sale in the *Staffordshire Advertiser* of 25th September 1874. The house is described as a capital messuage or mansion with outbuildings, garden and pleasure grounds. It was purchased by Alfred Sohier Bolton on 24th March 1875. The purchase price seems to have been £26,500 including the timber as Mr Charles Blagg, the Cheadle solicitor went to Warrington (home of J.W. Patten, then Baron Winmarleigh) to arrange the purchase on these terms on 5th September 1874. (4) Extensions at Moor Court, Oakamoor, saw the Bolton family moving to Lightoaks on 15th June 1878. An entry in Alfred Bolton's diary records, "All slept at Lightoaks for the first time". Thomas and Nina Bolton (Alfred's oldest son and his wife) took up residence at Lightoaks on 4th December 1880, presumably whilst Oakamoor Lodge was being made ready for their move there in May 1881. On the night of the census of 1881, Alfred Bolton and his family, together with son Thomas and his wife Nina, were in residence at Lighoaks Hall. Their domestic staff included a German-born tutor, two nurses, a cook, three housemaids, a kitchen-maid, a butler, a groom and a page. Kelly's *Directory* of 1892 records Major General Thomas William Sneyd, JP living at Lightoaks.

Lightoaks was in the Boltons' possession until recently: the last of the Bolton family to occupy the house was Tom, the great grandson of Alfred Bolton; he died in 2002. The house was originally much smaller and was later extended, probably by A.S. Bolton. It is possible that it was the principal residence of John Wilson Patten. His main house, Bank Hall, in Warrington was sold in 1872 to Warrington Council for £22,000 and became the Town Hall. (5)

See also Oakamoor Lodge (p.111) and Moor Court (p.109).

Lightoaks as constructed and (below) as later extended

Longton Hall, Longton, Stoke-on-Trent

Demolished

In 1702 Obadiah Lane rebuilt an earlier hall, acquired from Lord Foley, in an Italianate style. (1) Richard Foley is recorded as "of Longton Hall" in 1608. In the 1770s Richard Edensor Heathcote purchased the hall, reconstructing it into an imposing Georgian country house. Longton Hall was an elegant,white three-storeyed house set in a small park with a large, oval lawn and a pool. Longton Hall remained in the ownership of the Heathcote family until 1928. (2) The hall was tenanted at various times. From the early 1830s to at least 1851 Charles Harvey, a Longton banker, lived here.(3) In 1861 Henry Wileman, a local pottery manufacturer, was the tenant. He lived at the hall with his wife Ann and two servants. Longton Hall was finally sold by the Heathcote executors to the Wootons in 1933 and demolished in 1939. (4) Longton Hall was situated about a mile to the north of Blurton.

Longton Hall from the park in 1843 (Ward)

Loxley Hall, nr Uttoxeter

School

The Kinnersley family were established at Loxley since the 14th century. They lived in an earlier hall which may have been remodelled in c. 1607. The hall pictured here was built c. 1800 although it contained elements from an earlier building, having a date in a frieze of 1607. Clement Kinnersley, who died in 1815, bequeathed the hall to his nephew Thomas Sneyd. He was the son of John Sneyd of Belmont. Thomas added the surname Kinnersley to satisfy the terms of his uncle's will. Loxley Hall is a large, late Georgian house of three storeys. Pevsner described it as a large property with an eleven-bay ashlar front and a porch with four Tuscan columns. He described an entrance hall as being 40ft x 24ft wide and 30ft high and having a curious relic of old wainscoting, embellished with paintings in panels. They depicted "The Saviour", "The Flight into Egypt", "The Apostles and Evangelists" and "The Last Supper". There was a frieze or cornice of the arms of the royal family of about the year 1607. Pevsner also described a large staircase with twisted balusters in William and Mary style and a stable yard with a large octagonal brick dovecote.

Although Loxley Hall is identified as the seat of the Kinnersleys, they did not always live there and the hall was tenanted throughout much of the 19th and early 20th century. (1) However, Mrs Sneyd-Kinnersley lived there during the Great War and Italian prisoners of war and American servicemen occupied the hall during the Second World War. In 1945 Staffordshire County Council bought the hall and in 1954 it became a school for boys with special educational needs. Its situated on the Uttoxeter – Weston Road.

Loxley Hall in 1798 (Shaw)

Maer Hall, Maer

Reduced

The hall was built in c. 1680 and sold in 1693 to Captain John Chetwynd. In the same year Walter Chetwynd of Ingestre died and John Chetwynd left Maer to live there. John Chetwynd, junior, succeeded at Maer (he was born in 1680 and was the younger brother of Walter, Viscount Chetwynd). Maer passed to the Talbot family from Viscount Chetwynd. In 1790 it was sold to a member of the Bent family, who sold it in 1804 to Josiah Wedgwood II for £30,000. He borrowed the money from Robert Darwin, the father of Charles Darwin. (1) Wedgwood moved to Maer in 1807. (2)

Wedgwood converted the hall into an elegant mansion and embellished the grounds with plantations. (3) His daughter, Emma, married Charles Darwin and it is reputed that Charles wrote the *Origin of Species* while staying at the hall.

Josiah died at Maer in 1843 followed by his wife, Bessy, in 1846. William Davenport then bought the estate, almost rebuilding the house and adding a morning room, billiard room and clock tower. He also added extensive stabling. (4) Davenport died at Maer Hall in 1869; his son, Henry, succeeded him. He lived there until 1880 and the hall was then tenanted. The tenant in 1881 was Armar H.L. Corry. He employed twelve servants to care for himself, his wife and two young children. The owner after the Davenports was Frederic James Harrison, a Liverpool shipowner. He bought the hall and 3,500 acres in 1892 and spent a great deal of money on modernizing the interior. He added a new entrance at the northern end, enclosed the courtyard to form a great hall and installed electric light. After the modernisation, the hall had 65 rooms (including secondary rooms) and five staircases connected by corridors and passageways. (5) After Frederic's death his daughters lived at the hall. In 1963, after the death of Miss Jeanette Harrison, the estate was broken up and auctioned in July 1964. It extended to 900 acres. Dr J.M. Tellwright bought the hall and had demolished the Victorian extensions by 1972. Maer Hall was sold to Mr B.J. Fradley in 1980.

The Victorian addition from the north, which has now been removed

The left side has now been removed, returning the house to its appearance prior to the Victorian additions

Moor Court, Oakamoor

Residential Care Centre

The home of Alfred S. Bolton from 1862 until his death in 1901. He was the senior partner in Thomas Bolton & Sons, copper manufacturers of Oakamoor. Although built by him, he was unable to purchase the freehold from the Earl of Shrewsbury. In 1875 A.S. Bolton proposed an exchange of land but his land turned out to be worth £1,700 less than that of the Earl. The Earl, in any event, would not agree to an exchange in principle, but proposed a lease. A.S. Bolton suggested a 42-year lease with a ground rent with a review at 21 years. However, the Earl died on 11th May 1877, aged 47 years. It was exactly another year before the lease was signed.

It must have been frustrating for one of the country's leading copper manufacturers to be unable to secure the freehold on his pleasant home, but that remained the case. A.S. Bolton's diary reveals that on 3rd August 1860, "Critchlow delivered 1st load of stone from Alton Park on land in Farley Lane for my new house'. On 8th April 1861, he recorded: 'Began to make bricks in Farley Lane again this season". No doubt bricks were delivered to the new house site as well as Oakamoor Mills, Bolton's copper works. On 4th May he "Drove to Stubwood to see brickyard kept by Phillip [sic] Wright, which may indicate another source for the house. It is likely that much of the materials came from local sources, although the floor tiles were from Minton Hollins of Stoke-on-Trent. On 23 April, 1862 he noted, 'Slept in new house for 1st time.' The Farley Lane bricks would appear to have been made adjacent to the house. The architect was William Sugden, of Leek. (1)

The house was extended in 1878, the contract for the work being agreed at £1,365 with a Mr Fielding. The family moved to Lightoaks during the construction work. Francis (Frank) Bolton and his wife Connie were the first to occupy it on 7th January 1880; his father and mother moved back later. The architect for the extension was Larner Sugden, of Leek, son of William. The house was further extended by Frank Bolton in 1913. It remained in the Bolton family as a home until the latter's death in 1951.

In c. 1955, it was purchased by the Home Office as a Women's Correction Centre. It was subsequently sold and is now Moorcare, a residential home for people with learning difficulties, founded by Peter Thornley who bought it in 1990.

Pevsner described the house as a "neo-Jacobean house with shaped gables". Several members of the Bolton family are buried in Oakamoor churchyard.

Moor Court in 1861

Above: Another view from 1861

Below: The house following alterations

Oakamoor Lodge, Oakamoor

Demolished

This house was built for George Kendall in 1761. He was an early industrialist in this area and ran an iron rolling mill and a tin plating works in Oakamoor. Tin plate consisted of rolled iron coated in a thin layer of tin. Coincidentally, a description of this works was made in 1761 by J.L. Robshsahm, a Swedish industrialist. Kendal had interests in several ironworks, one of which is preserved at Furnace, on the Machynlleth to Aberystwyth road, dating from 1755. In c. 1780, Kendal sold the Oakamoor works to the firm of Smith and Knifton and George Smith appears to have purchased Oakamoor Lodge at the same time. (1)

In the early 1800s, the Wragge family occupied the house, but it appears to have been purchased by the Cheadle Copper and Brass Company in 1828 when they also purchased the Oakamoor mill. In that year, George Wragge (junior) was a partner in the Cheadle Company earning £200 p.a., plus free occupation of the house. Occupied in 1834 by Mrs Emma Wragge, it was purchased in 1852 apparently by John Wilson Patten, Baron Winmarleigh, whose family controlled the Cheadle company. He sold both Oakamoor Lodge and Lightoaks to the Boltons in c. 1875. Alfred Bolton had purchased the Oakamoor Copper Works in 1852 from the Cheadle Company. Both Lightoaks and Oakamoor Lodge were offered for sale on 25th September 1874 by auction at Cheadle. At that time the latter was tenanted by Miss Harriet Ramsay. The estate consisted of 330 acres, plus 15 cottages in addition to Lightoaks and Oakamoor Lodge and was sold as one lot.

Alfred Bolton's oldest son, Thomas, married Nina Rathbone of Liverpool in 1880 and having moved temporarily into Lightoaks, moved on to Oakamoor Lodge on 21st May 1881. They lived here until 1893 before returning to Lightoaks.

Oakamoor Lodge

Tom and his wife separated in 1901, the same year as his sister Sarah Beatrice married Dr Peter Bearblock, who became the works doctor at Oakamoor Mills. In 1902 they moved in and they lived there until their deaths, in 1948 and 1951 respectively. Their son married in the early 1950s and left Oakamoor. In 1953, the empty house was demolished. (2) It was situated across the road from the railway station.

Oakamoor Railway Station, with Oakamoor Lodge to the left

Okeover Hall, Okeover

Rebuilt

Much has been written on the current house with good articles in *Country Life* alone. (1) However, although this building has been remodelled from time to time, as shown in the photographs included here, our emphasis is on an enchanting earlier house, which was set in the middle of a moat. Fortunately, a drawing of this house as it was in c. 1660 exists. (2)

The building is relatively simple in style, although the drawing seems to suggest that the ground floor windows are unusually high above the simple garden. There is no symmetry to this south front at all. Judging by the chimneys rising above the ridge of the roof of the south front, the house looks as though it was possibly built with four fronts around a courtyard. The clue would seem to be two small chimneys or roof features, which could be above a north front – unless two wings projected from the building illustrated.

This house was replaced, but the church remains, although altered in the Victorian era. Behind it is another building on the site of the current stable block. Set in its island site, a wall/fence enclosing the moat and with the timber of the deer park reaching almost to the house, the whole scene encapsulates a style that still survives at Little Moreton Hall in Cheshire.

The stream, which fed the moat, may be seen draining away in the foreground. It survives in the park to the south-east of the current house – or at least the bed of it, for the water table appears to have dropped.

The occupier of this house in the 1660s was Rowland Okeover.

Okeover in 1686 (Plot)

This page and opposite: Views of the south front of the current house prior to alterations

The house today, with virtually the whole south front rebuilt

Parker House, 2 Church Street, Leek

Shops

This substantial stone-built house incorporates the remains of a 16th century timber-framed building. (1) The house, pictured here was built by Thomas Parker, who retained what was structurally sound of the old house and rebuilt round it. (2) The house had four rooms on the upper floors and three on the ground floor. There was also an access passage to the stable yard leading to a purpose built stable. (3)

Parker's son, also Thomas, was born here in 1666; he was called to the bar in 1691 and was appointed Lord Chief Justice in 1710. He was created Baron Parker of Macclesfield in 1716 and became Lord Chancellor of Great Britain in 1718. Created Earl of Macclesfield in 1721, he was impeached for corruption in 1725 and found guilty. (4) Thomas Parker was removed from office, taken to the Tower and sentenced to pay a fine of £30,000. (5) The house remained one property until at least 1881 when members of the Critchlow family had lived there for several years. By 1891 a lock-up shop adjoined the house. In 1908, no. 2 was still a family home while no. 4 was an accountant's office.

Arthur Cecil Parker, grandson of the 6th Earl of Macclesfield, was at no. 4 in 1912, where he ran the estate office. This handsome house has been divided into two shop premises for almost a hundred years.

Above & opposite: Three views of 2, Church Street, the home of Sir Thomas Parker

The house, adjoining Foxlowe, then also a private house. The building on the right of the photograph was the Golden Lion Hotel. The railings on the left are around the garden of the vicarage

Paynsley Hall, Draycott in the Moors

Demolished

The Department of the Environment listing of 1986 states that this was a 16th century farmhouse, refaced in the 17th century. It was extended in the early 19th century and was then (1986) derelict. It consisted of red brick with a timber frame with tiled roof. The 19th century additions dominated the earlier house. The lower 16th century portion was attached to the right of the later and larger extension. It comprised a single bay cross wing, a gabled building parallel to the 19th century part, belonging to a house which was probably of a hall and cross wing type running at right angles to the remaining block.

In 1986, an interior and side wall of herringbone bracing in five panels was exposed (see photograph). A roof truss of collared type and with double purlins was visible where the hall ridge was attached.

It is a pity that this venerable building was allowed to decay to the point that it collapsed. The photographs reproduced here give some idea of what it looked like in the 1920s, when it was occupied as a farmhouse. The occupier from 1910–26 was W.G. Vernon. The other photographs portray the derelict building.

The house shortly before it collapsed

Above: Paynsley in c. 1928

Below: The house deteriorated rapidly after it became disused. This was taken in c. 1960

Three views from the 1960s. The bottom photograph (taken after the structure collapsed) shows some of the herringbone studding. High on one wall on the first floor was a stone plaque with the Ten Commandments, believed to be on the interior wall of the large chimney stack. The latter was part of the original structure

Rolleston Hall, Rolleston-on-Dove

Mostly demolished

Edward Mosley bought the Hall in 1622 from the Rollestons. Local historians believe that it was probably of timber construction and by 1665, the date of the Hearth Tax, it was occupied by a farmer called Bond and was described as demolished. This may indicate the rebuilding of the house at that time. A hall was owned by an Oswald Mosley in the 18th century who employed Thomas Gardener of Uttoxeter to improve the house prior to his death in 1789.

Kelly's Post Office Directory of 1860 described Rolleston as " a handsome modern building on a very ancient site, surrounded by a park of 300 acres with fine gardens and pleasure grounds with many rare pines and valuable trees. It was the seat of Sir Oswald Mosley. The house was badly damaged by fire in 1871 and a large Italianate mansion was built onto the shell of the old house in 1872-3. The older house is shown on a painting of 1838 (see below, from a private collection) and on another of 1846. The latter is recorded in a photograph held by the National Monuments record (NMR) at Swindon. The NMR has a collection of photographs taken inside the rebuilt house, some of which are reproduced here (Bedford Lemere Collection). (1)

Following the succession of the 6th Baronet, Sir Oswald in the early 1920s, the Mosley estate was sold in the mid 1920s. The majority of the hall was demolished in November 1925 after various unsuccessful auction sales to sell it either as one large house or as flats. The only remaining portions are the Ballroom (now converted into a two storey house called The Paddock) and a single storey wing built in 1870 as Sir Tonman Mosley's private apartments, later used as the estate office and now known as The Old Hall.

(http://www.rolleston-on-dove.freeserve.co.uk/history.htm)

Rolleston in 1838 (private collection)

*Above:
The Dining Room*

*Below: Lady
Moseley's Bedroom*

*Opposite top:
The Moorish Room*

*Opposite bottom:
The Drawing Room*

Left: The Main Staircase

Below: Rolleston Hall. The nature of the event is unknown. Ninety-eight people are shown here. This shows part of the rebuilt house

Rushton Grange, N.W. of Cobridge, Stoke-on-Trent

Demolished

Rushton Grange was in the parish of Burslem and was once a grange to Hulton Abbey. It was granted in 1539 to James Leveson who immediately sold it to Richard Biddulph for £130. 7s. The Biddulph family were Roman Catholics and the Parliamentary Committee for the County of Stafford sequestered the estate during the civil war. The Bagnalls, another Roman Catholic family, were tenants of Francis Biddulph. The Roman Catholics in the area used part of the farmhouse as a place of worship. Another tenant, John Bagnall, was forced to flee the house during the disturbances associated with the flight of James II in 1688 and the property was ransacked by a mob from the Burslem area. In the second half of the 17th and the 18th century the Biddulph family sold land on the east side of Rushton Grange and by the early 1840s the estate had been reduced to 220 acres.

Most of the land was let to William Gething, who was recorded in the 1851 census returns as the occupier of 103 acres on which he employed four agricultural labourers. By then the Grange farm had been divided into two with the other part occupied by William, who was a farm bailiff, his wife and an agricultural labourer. (www.thepotteries.org)

Rushton Grange in 1843 (Ward)

Shaw Hall, South of Kingsley
Demolished

Also known as Shaw Hall, The Shaw(e) and The Booth (Hall).

At the beginning of the 18th century, an older house was occupied by the Stubbs family. (1) They may have been tenants, for this house was part of the Shaw estate and was owned by Sir Joseph Banks. It was sold in 1790 and purchased by James Beech, the son of John Beech, who was probably the tenant. He died on 20th October 1787 and is described in the Kingsley Church Register as being "of the Shaw, Sqier". The estate fetched £3,300 and it is clear that James Beech had difficulties paying for it and for some time after the disposal sale. Included with the estate was the Lordship of the Manor of Kingsley.

The house, pictured below, was built in 1821 by John Beech. It consisted of a central block with a pedimented front. James Beech died in 1828 and his son, also James, inherited. In both 1834 and 1851 the house was unoccupied, the owner (this James Beech) being described as being of Brandon, near Coventry. (2) At the time of the 1881 census the house was occupied by the head gardener, William Wainwright and his wife Mary, who was the housekeeper, together with their son who was the under gardener.

In 1919 a sale catalogue described The Shaw with its pleasure grounds, park, fish ponds and home pastures. The ground floor had dining, drawing, morning, billiard and smoking rooms. There were also a housekeeper's room, kitchen, scullery, two larders and a china closet, a butler's pantry, a servants' hall, a wash house and a lamp room,

The first floor could be reached by two staircases and had seven principal bedrooms and two dressing rooms. There was also eight servants bedrooms, a house maids closet, three front attics, a boxroom and a tank room.

Outside were stables, with five stalls, three loose boxes, a washing box, two coach houses, a saddle room, with men's room, a storeroom and lofts.

The outbuildings comprised sheds, a carpenter's shop, a keeper's room and a stick house.A walled kitchen garden is also mentioned. In 1919, The Shaw was still part of the Beech estates.

By 1960 the house was ruinous and one wonders if this was due to coal mining subsidence. It was demolished in 1987. (3) The Old Hall owned by Sir Joseph Banks was else-where (now demolished.

Shaw Hall, showing the entrance front

Swythamley Hall, Heaton

Apartments

Swythamley Hall was the ancient seat of the Trafford family, granted to the family in 1540 by Henry VIII. The Victoria County History of Staffordshire, vol VII informs us that it was assessed for tax on eight hearths in 1666 and possibly remodelled in the 1690s. A section of wall incorporated in the present west front may be from the 17th century house, and it appears to have formed the south-west corner of what by the late 18th century was an irregular double-pile house. The house was damaged by fire in 1813, although parts then added by Edward Nicholls survived. (1) This may explain why a sale notice dated 1831 described Swythamley as 'recently erected of stone in the most beautiful part of the park'. It was spacious, comfortable and convenient having a library, breakfast room, dining and drawing rooms, a kitchen and a servants' hall on the ground floor. The dining and drawing rooms communicated by large, folding mahogany doors. Outside were stables with boxes for 12 horses, a coach house and dog kennels. The 80-acre park was enclosed by walls and was well stocked with deer. The woods and plantations contained oak, alder and ash trees. The extensive 3,000-acre estate was stocked with black game.

John Brocklehurst of Macclesfield bought the hall in 1832. His son William succeeded him in 1839, though he mainly resided at Macclesfield. (2) The Brocklehursts enlarged the house and by 1862 a canted bay had been added to the room at the south-west corner and there was a billiard room at the north end. The billiard room stood on the west side of what had been an open courtyard, on whose other sides were service quarters. The courtyard was covered over by Philip Brocklehurst, circa 1860, for use as a dining room and ballroom, by the tenants, at the twice-yearly estate audit. The service quarters were removed in the early 20th century, when a large two-storeyed porch was added to the west front. The outbuildings north-east of the house include a late 18th century stable block, enlarged in 1860 to enclose a yard, and a tenants' hall of 1888. (3) On the night of the census in 1881 only servants were in residence at the hall. A directory dated 1896 described Swythamley as a long, irregular stone building, covered with ivy, in a deer park of 200 acres. Owned at the time by Philip Lancaster Brocklehurst, it overlooked a great extent of wild scenery. The Brocklehursts and their descendants owned the hall until 1977 when it was sold to the World Government for the Age of Enlightenment, followers of an Indian mystic, Maharishi Mahesh Yogi. In 1987 it was sold to Mr R.M. Naylor, who divided the house and outbuildings into a number of separate residential units.

The original house on an 1831 estate plan

The house was twice extended post-1831 as may be seen on these two views

Throwley Hall, west of Ilam

Ruinous, mostly demolished

"Throwley is very much a private world." So wrote Faith Cleverdon in 1995 and indeed she was so right. (1) Her book, published by the City Museum, Hanley, Stoke-on-Trent, is recommended to all those interested in her archaeological survey work either side of the Manifold Valley between Beeston Tor and Ilam. It is a fascinating insight into man's early settlement here. In the middle of this area are the ruins of Throwley Hall.

Its ruinous state may be traced back to the marriage of Elizabeth, daughter of the last of the Meverells, to Thomas Cromwell, 4th Baron Cromwell and eventually created the Earl of Ardglass. Thereafter, reduced to the status of a dower house, the building seems to have been largely unlived in by the owner, although it was let to two tenants (i.e. two households) from at least the early 18th century.

Cleverdon states (2) that the house was once the centre of a small village of at least nine households, farming an area of 1,435 acres. She traces the history of the property back to 1208 when Oliver Meverell purchased land there. The house was certainly there in the early 14th century. The house seems to have been remodelled by Sampson Meverell, perhaps in 1603, although Pevsner stated that he preferred a date of early 16th century. Paul Everson, writing in Cleverdon's book, (3) suggests that it is more likely that a crosswing of a late medieval building was incorporated into a 16th century house, with the surviving (but now ruined) tower added a century or so later. By the late 18th century (1779) a survey for a prospective buyer noted that the house would need improvement and perhaps equally important, the area was "thin of people, especially Gentlemen".

In 1790, the estate, by then having passed to Edward Southwell, was sold to Sir Samuel Crompton. Between 1838 and 1878, the current Hall was built and the old house left to decay. (4)

The remaining part is only a small portion of the original house, probably pulled down between 1846, when it was described by Hall, (5) and 1882, when Niven described the house as only having a wing remaining. (6) Looking at the site from the public road, one sees the rear of the house; the main entrance faced the valley, on the north side. Until recently, the only early illustrations of the house have been Hall's engraving of 1846, an interesting rear view of c. 1900 and a few Edwardian photographs showing the ruined remains. However, another photograph taken by Alice Hurt has survived. A very early, keen photographer, her father's diary records her travelling to Casterne with him from Alderwasley Hall in June 1858, where she took a photograph. The diary records that the photographic cart went ahead! It is likely that this photograph was taken on the same day, for all the images in the surviving album appear to be of a similar date (some dated 1861). (7) Certainly, it would appear from this photograph that most of the house had gone when it was taken.

The remains are now scheduled as an Ancient Monument and have been stabilised. Some panelling was apparently removed to Wootton Lodge and some glass and panelling has been incorporated into the new hall.

The house in 1846 (top) and in 1858, when taken by Alice Hurt

The north side of the house c. 1900, taken by Mr Potter of Ashbourne

Left: Throwley in 1910

Below & opposite: The stabilised remains today

Trentham Hall, Trentham

Mostly demolished

Charles Barry remodelled this magnificent mansion, in 1834, for the 2nd Duke of Sutherland. Barry also laid out Italian gardens to the front of the hall. The huge Italianate style house was built in two phases in the 1830s and 1840s at a total cost of £123,000. Pevsner considered it as important as the Houses of Parliament. The Leveson-Gower family resided there until the beginning of the 20th century. On the night of the census in 1901 only Rosemary Leveson-Gower, the Duke's seven-year-old daughter, was in residence. She had the company of a teacher and 32 servants who included a schoolroom maid and 16 grooms. In the hunt stables were 12 other grooms. One of the reasons the Duke gave for closing the hall, in 1905, was the appalling smell from the river. In 1910 the Duke of Sutherland offered the hall to the County of Staffordshire and the Borough of Stoke-on-Trent. The offer was refused and the building was demolished, apart from the west front and stable block.

There was a house in Plot's time (1686), built by the Levesons, replaced in the early 18th century by a house designed by Francis Smith. This was in turn enlarged by Capability Brown and Holland in 1768–78 at the same time as the lake. Contrary to Pevsner's usual style of ignoring demolished buildings, he spends some time describing Barry's work here, which is recommended. (1) The site is now occupied by Trentham Gardens. There is currently a proposal to convert the remaining buildings into a five-star hotel.

Trentham, as rebuilt by Barry

Above: The Georgian classical fronted house Middle & bottom: Scenes of Trentham in 1686 (Plot)

Westwood Hall, Westwood Park Road, Leek

School

This was a major grange existing in the Middle Ages. In 1813 John Davenport, a potter and glassmaker of Longport, purchased the hall, together with Westwood Farm and Wallbridge Farm for £1,380. Davenport was responsible for improving the neglected Westwood Estate and refurbishing the house. (1) By 1834 the house was known as Westwood Hall and described as a neat mansion with extensive plantations and pleasure grounds. Working with architect James Eames, Davenport added a new south entrance front and a wing to the north-east. This enlarged house had two storeys with attics and was of Elizabethan style with curved gables and mullioned and transomed windows.

John Davenport laid out a terraced lawn to the east of the house, entrance gates to the south-east and a Gothic outbuilding with tower and spire to the south-west. He died in 1848. In 1851 John Davenport, junior, extended the hall and built a great hall and tower at the west end of the south front together with extensive buildings around a courtyard on the north-west. These extensions in a plain Elizabethan style, by Weighton, Hadfield and Goldie of Sheffield, were of stone on the principal elevations and of red brick elsewhere. The surviving elevations by Eames were altered to match.

The lodge was built in 1852. There was another on the Newcastle Road near Wallbridge. Both survive. (2) Kelly's *Post Office Directory* of 1860 lists John Davenport of Westwood Hall, but he died just two years later in 1862.

On 6th August 1862 Westwood Hall and Dieulacres Abbey Estates, comprising the hall, two water corn mills, Bowling Green Inn, School (sic) cottages, and 2,156 acres of land in total were offered for sale at Crewe. (3) The hall was described as a very commodious mansion of red sandstone in the Elizabethan style of architecture. The rooms included a music hall, study, entrance hall, morning room, dining room, boudoir, bedrooms and dressing rooms, bathroom, housekeeper's room, servants' hall, brushing room, scullery, kitchen, larder and butler's pantry. The detailed inventory of the contents of the house shows that the bedrooms and dressing rooms attached were given names; they included the Pine, Heath, Fir Cone and Tower. There was also a room designated for "bachelors".

The hall failed to sell in 1862 and the hall and gardens were advertised to let in 1866 and were leased to James Watts in 1867. In 1868 John Robinson bought the hall and the remainder of the estate which had not sold in 1862. Growing timber and all the mansion house furnishing and fittings were included in the sale price of £50,000. (4)

John Robinson maintained the hall in good order throughout the rest of his life. On the night of the census in 1881 he was living at Westwood with his wife and four adult children, six domestic servants, a groom and an undergardener. John Robinson gives his occupation as JP for Staffordshire and a member of the Institute of Civil Engineers. He died in 1902 leaving his wife Helen to live at Westwood. Helen died in 1908 and her three sons sold the hall in 1909 to Henry James Johnson, Esq. The hall, gardens and grounds at this time comprised 96 acres. Henry Johnson was a china manufacturer and he and his family lived at Westwood until it was sold in 1920.

The County Council bought the hall in 1920 and it opened as a girls' high school in 1921. The land sold amounted to 14 acres and the price was £15,500. The intake comprised the older girls from the mixed Leek County High School at the Nicholson Institute and the older pupils from the Church High School for girls at the Maude institute. In 1965 the school was merged with the newly built St Edward's C. of E. (aided) Secondary School in Westwood Park Avenue to form a mixed comprehensive school.

Above: Westwood prior to extentions (Sleigh)
Below: The house after 1851

Above: A social gathering at the house Below: The Lodge, Westwood Road

Woodcroft, Newcastle Road, Leek

Demolished

In 1921, a sale notice in the *Leek Times* described Woodcroft as a substantially built house standing well back from the (Newcastle) road. It had three reception rooms, an oak-panelled billiard room, nine bedrooms, two bathrooms, a tower room and a box room. Outside were stabling for three horses, a harness room and a coach house. The house was surrounded by three acres of beautiful gardens with a tennis court, shady lawn and a productive kitchen garden.

This house dates from the early 1880s. The Sugden firm of architects designed alterations to this property in 1891 but it is not known if these were carried out. Henry Davenport and his wife Eliza lived here in the early 1890s; he was a silk manufacturer from the firm of Wardle and Davenport. His widow, Eliza still lived at Woodcroft in 1899. By 1924, John and Ethel Shorter lived here; he was the managing director of Wardle and Davenport. During the later 1930s a private estate had been built north of the Newcastle road over the site and grounds of Woodcroft and over the grounds of Woodcroft Grange.

Woodhead Hall, Cheadle

An earlier hall was assessed for four hearths in 1665 and another hall was built in 1719 by Mr William Leigh. (1) Edward Leigh, Esquire, died in 1751 aged 52 and his wife Ann in July 1742 aged 61. In 1758 Francis Leigh lived at the hall. When this property was sold in 1820 it was described as a capital mansion house called Woodhead with coach house, stables, out-buildings, yards, walled garden, plantations and shrubberies. A Captain Honeyburn sold it to Mr Thompson who was living at the hall in 1834. (2) Thomas Thompson lived at the hall with his family in 1841. However it was bought by William Allen in that year. (3) The 1845 pew allotments of Cheadle Church state that William Allen had ten sittings in pew 8 in the south gallery. At this time pew sittings were attached to specific houses and passed from one owner to the next.

William Allen, a successful merchant, died in 1871 and his wife Maria, nee Shepherd, in 1870 (his monument is in Cheadle churchyard). Their son, William Shepherd Allen, decided to demolish and rebuild the hall when extensive dry rot was discovered there in 1871. (4) He was Member of Parliament for Newcastle-under-Lyme from 1865 to 1886. In 1871 the occupants of Woodhead had "gone to London for the season".

Sugden built the present Woodhead Hall, on a slightly higher position, in 1873. It was built in red brick and sandstone in an Italianate style. There were 28 rooms, half used by the family and half by servants. (5) This new hall was almost square 85 feet by 80 feet. It was a double-fronted building with attics and cellars. Sandstone pillars flanked the entrance doors and the large central hallway beyond contained a pine staircase illuminated by a glass roof. (6)

According to burial records, William Shepherd Allen (1831–1913) lived here with his wife Penelope (1847–1922). Their children were born at Woodhead.

In 1925 the hall was leased to the Misses Hunt as a home and preparatory school (7) After the lease expired in 1936 the Air Ministry rented it for use as a wireless station. During World War II it was occupied by service personnel and several unsightly extentions were added. A new roof was added in 1985; at this time it was owned by the Crown Agents who sold it in 1995. Woodhead Hall has been bought by the Chesters family who have restored it to its original condition and demolished the unsightly extentions. The house is a family home once more after many years of other uses.

Wootton Hall, Ellastone

Demolished

Wootton occupied a site just north of Ellastone with lovely views to the Dove Valley and beyond. It seems to have been built in 1730 by the Bromley Davenports, who demolished it in 1935.

Surviving illustrations show that it occupied a sloping site. The south front was three storeys, the middle floor being at ground level on the north side. The main block on the south front consisted of two bays on either side of a three-storey bow (actually three-sided, not rounded) with a wrought iron balcony at first floor level. The south-west corner projected with a Venetian window at the first floor together with another, longer, balcony in front of the latter window. The west side of this corner looked down onto Rousseau's cave and the terrace above it. A terraced garden adjoined the south front with a row of urns on square stone pedestals on the terrace wall. A clock tower existed on the south-east corner.

The west front had what appeared to be an extra storey, but was probably three-storey, standing on higher ground. The roof was mostly flat, at least over the main rooms, with a pierced balustrade, not dissimilar to the garden wall adjoining the south front at Calwich. The house appears to have been built with stone, with ashlar surrounds to the windows and projecting corners of the walls.

The house from the terrace, showing the south front

Put up for sale in 1924, it failed to sell and was again auctioned on 16th May 1929 at the Green Man Hotel, Ashbourne, but failed to sell. At the demolition sale, the staircase and ashlar surround to Rousseau's cave went to Mr W. Podmore of Consall Hall in 1935. Much stone went to rebuild Hanging Bridge, Mayfield and further bits and pieces were incorporated into a bungalow, which still exists opposite The George in Waterhouses, on the corner of the road to Waterfall.

In 1862, the house was owned by Lt. Col. W. Bromley Davenport, MP for North Warwickshire. He had succeeded on the death of his father Rev. Walter Davenport in that year. However, the house by then had changed since Rousseau's occupation almost 100 years before. In the 1850s, it underwent change. Rooms occupied by Rousseau had been removed to make way for a new entrance hall. (1) Presumably this entrance hall incorporated a new staircase, sold to Mr W. Podmore and still in use at Consall Hall.

Wootton Hall is renowned for being the home for about a year or so of Jean-Jacques Rousseau. Persuaded by sympathisers to leave his exile in Switzerland and come to England, he arrived in London early in 1766 with Térèse Le Vasseur, his companion. He shortly proceeded to Wootton, arriving there in April 1766. His friends arranged for him to take an apartment there for £30p.a. Unfortunately his time there could have been happier. Rousseau is described as having an irritable and suspicious nature. (2)

Although he was settled enough to write the first six books of his *Confessions* whilst at Wootton, his companion, who seems to have spoken no English, became tired of living there. She appears to have conspired to cause him to leave, preying upon his irrationality. He was to leave for Spalding without his possessions; where he wanted a guard to escort him to Dover. It was unfortunate that Rousseau decided to leave in such a hasty manner. His fellow philosopher and friend, Mr Hume reportedly said that "Mr Davenport tells me he intends to leave our friend [Rousseau] the life-rent of the house in which he lives, if he finds that his attachment to it continues". (3)

Close to the west front of the house was a small room excavated in the adjacent sandstone and with a door set in ashlar masonry. Apparently Rousseau used this room and it became known as Rousseau's cave. The remains of the 'cave' still survive at Wootton.

This book is about former houses but Wootton's history took an unexpected turn. In 2000, the Hon. Johnny Greenall and his wife Laura applied for planning permission to rebuild a new house on the site of Wootton Hall. A new country seat rose on the foundations of the former house, a site abandoned for nearly 70 years. It is built in traditional style and with traditional materials – of stone and slate, the former coming from a quarry on the Duke of Devonshire's estate. By a fortunate twist of fate, Mrs Greenall is a member of the Duncombe family, who held nearby Calwich Abbey until that was also demolished in 1935. It is with some gratification that your authors are able to record the renaissance of Wootton Hall when completed in 2002 (above).

Above: Another view of the south front, from below the two terraces

Below: The north front, showing the entrance, redesigned in the 1850s

Rousseau's Cave in situ at Wootton (left) and at Consall (above right)
Below: The new Wooton Hall, showing the south and east fronts

Yoxall Lodge, Newchurch

Demolished

Originally one of several hunting lodges built in Needwood Forest. Nearby was Byrkley Lodge, later the home of Lord Bass, and also demolished. Some of the plantations on the 800 acre Yoxall Lodge estate were residual parts of this ancient estate.

In the 18th century, the house was rebuilt, probably with brick. The foundations of one of the east front bays survive and are of brick. In the late 18th century, it was the home of Rev. Thomas Gisborne (1758–1846), who had inherited it from his father. He was a poet and collector of botanical specimens. In 1794 he published a book of poems called *Walks in a Forest*. The British Museum has twenty volumes of preserved specimens of over 600 species of plants collected by him at Yoxall Lodge chiefly in 1790–92. William Wilberforce was apparently a frequent visitor, using the house as a retreat to work on the abolition of the slave trade. He was encouraged by Thomas Babington, the brother of Gisborne's wife.

In 1851 Thomas Gisborne farmed 800 acres here; he described himself as a landowner, collier and limeburner who employed 200 labourers. A directory of 1908 listed a Mrs Griffiths as resident at Yoxall Lodge. She was the widow of Guy Gisborne, Esq, who had married John Harewood Griffiths. The house remained in the Gisborne family for most of the 19th century. It fell into disrepair in the early 20th century and joined several other houses in North Staffordshire in being demolished in 1935.

Today, the site of the house is occupied by a modern bungalow, the home of Mr and Mrs R. Featherstone. In 2005 they opened their farmland for the first time to view the millions of bluebells. These thrive in the relict woodlands, where they have lain undisturbed for centuries. There are three short trails to explore, which are recommended. Ring 01283 575237 for details.

The above text is based upon information received with thanks from Mr and Mrs Featherstone, who also provided the photographs.

Yoxall Lodge

Yoxall Lodge from the park and lake and a view of the walled garden

Part 2: More Memories

Birdsgrove House, Mayfield

This imposing house was built circa 1850 and was the seat of Mrs Sarah Greaves. (*White's Directory*, op. cit., 1851) By 1861 it was the home of Marcus Wright and his Finnish born wife, Fredrigne (sic). Marcus must have been a wealthy man of independent means as the enumerator recorded that he had no profession. Four servants occupied the house on the night of the 1871 census as the Wrights were visiting Caernarvonshire at the time. The Wrights' servants included a butler, cook, lady's maid, housemaid and a coachman. Marcus died at Birdsgrove in 1882 and is buried in St Martin's churchyard, Osmaston. His wife continued to reside at the house and was still there, aged 84, in 1901. The house later became a convalescent home for The Royal Pharmaceutical Society.

Brow Hill House, Clerk Bank, Leek

Demolished

Brow Hill was built just after 1838 and before the mid-1840s, for Robert Hammersley, a local silk dyer. It was three storeys high (sic), with four principal rooms on each floor. Purchased by Leek UDC in 1959 it was demolished and the site was used for council houses. Built above the upper end of Macclesfield Road, it had extensive gardens, stables and a carriage house.

Chartley Hall, near Stowe-by Chartley

Destroyed by fire

The original moated timber mansion house at Chartley was home to the Devereux family, who had moved from Chartley Castle during the 15th century. In 1575, Elizabeth I was entertained at Chartley Hall on her journey through Staffordshire. Elizabeth also had Mary Queen of Scots held prisoner here between December 1585 and September 1586, before she was taken to Fotheringhay Castle in Northamptonshire for trial and execution. It was at Chartley that Mary received information from Anthony Babington about a plot to free her and overthrow the Queen. Chartley Hall was destroyed by fire in 1781; the present hall was built in an Elizabethan style in 1847. Pictured is the house in 1686 (Plot).

Dimsdale Old Hall

Demolished

The hall was home to the Brett family in the 16th century. (1) Originally a half-timbered Tudor building, which could still be seen at the rear. The front was Jacobean in style, built in brick, with pedimental gables and large chimney stacks. It was gutted by fire in 1895. (2) Little was left standing when the estate was sold in c. 1925 and restored. Dimsdale Hall was demolished in 1940 and today it is the address of Wolstanton Golf Club.

The Grange, Cheadle

This old house was built in 1493 and demolished in 1966

The Heybridge, between Upper & Lower Tean

This substantial property was built in 1813 as a family home for the Philips family.(Short G., *Around Cheadle*, 1994, p56) The occupier of the property in 1851 was John William Philips who was born at Heybridge in 1827. He was the senior partner in the firm of John and Nathaniel Philips & Co, tape manufacturers in Tean. John Philips later became a captain of the Cheadle Company of the 1st Volunteer Battalion of the North Staffordshire Regiment eventually gaining the rank of Major.(Penn, *Staffordshire and Shropshire*, 1908) Visitors at the house in 1851 included Francis and Arthur Hibbert who were most probably relatives as John Philips' mother was Letitia Hibbert. These young men were obviously from a privileged background as Francis was a gentleman cadet in the Royal Military College and Arthur described himself as a West India merchant. John Philips married Adelaide Louisa Buller in 1852 but she had died by 1871 leaving John with four young children including an 11-month-old son. John's household staff at that time included a governess, nurse, nurserymaid, laundrymaid, scullerymaid, kitchen maid, housemaids, footman, groom, cook, housekeeper and butler.The Philips family lived at Heybridge into the 20th century. The house was demolished in the 1950s.

Built in 1913 by the Philips family, they occupiled it until it was demolished in the 1950s

Madeley Manor, Madeley

Shown by Plot in 1686

The Mansion, Cheadle

Robert Plant, a colliery owner of Cheadle, built the Mansion in 1869. The property was extended in 1872.The Plant family lived in the rear of the building in a part known as Ebenezer Cottage or Villa. That the Mansion was an extensive building is demonstrated, in 1881, when Robert and his wife lived in the rear portion with their ten children, his mother-in-law and two servants. The front part was let out for dances, entertainments and private functions. John Slater later bought the Mansion and converted it into a number of flats and rooms to rent. (1) In 1978 it was sold to Staffordshire Moorlands District Council who demolished it and built senior citizens bungalows on the site.

Rangemoor, near Barton-under-Needwood

This grade II listed hall was built for the Bass family but retains an early 19th century core; it was the seat of Henry Barton in 1851 (*Whites Directory*). In 1872 it was described as a beautiful edifice in the Italian style in a picturesque and well wooded park, surrounded by tastefully laid out pleasure grounds.(*Kelly's Directory*). From at least 1860 it was the home of the Bass family of brewers. Michael Thomas Bass died at Rangemoor in 1884 and his son, Michael Arthur in 1909. They are buried in All Saint's churchyard, Rangemore. The Bass family had several visitors staying with them in 1881 including several ladies. This explains the six ladies maid's who were part of the staff of 39 servants at the hall on the night of the census. Michael Arthur became the 1st Baron Burton in 1886. He was a friend of Edward VII who visited him at Rangemore in 1902. Nellie Lisa Bass inherited Rangemore Hall and the title of Baroness Burton after the death of her father, in 1909. The hall became a boarding school in 1954. After the school closed, the hall stood empty for a number of years before being bought by GRR Properties and converted into eight luxury apartments.

Roaches House, Upperhulne

This house was formerly called Argyle House or Cottage. It was built in 1876 and had a date stone on an upper floor. This floor has been removed. The date stone still survives on a garage.(1) It is said that the wallabies of the Peak District came from a small private zoo in the grounds of Roaches House near Leek. Henry Courtney Brocklehurst established the zoo in the mid 1930s. During WW2 wallabies from the zoo were released into the wild and started to breed on the Roaches. Other sources say that the wallabies escaped.

Shelton Old Hall

It was an Elizabethan mansion and the seat of the Fenton family; the poet Elijah Fenton was born here in 1683. The house is shown here in 1843 as a stone and half-timbered mansion with gables which were partly thatched. It had a two-storey extension of stone or brick thought to date from the 17th century. The hall burned down in 1853. The Wedgwood fire engine was said to have been used to fight a fire at Shelton Old Hall on Sunday 22nd May 1853. It was also reported that there was a feud between the Etruria and Hanley Fire Brigades which resulted in a pond water battle between them, with very little water reaching the burning house!

Thornbury Hall, Lockwood Road

George Thornbury of Thornbury was assessed for three hearths in 1665. In 1667 it was the seat of William Thornberry (sic). (Speake R, *A history of Thornbury and Farley*, 1996). The house was offered for sale in 1832 (Chester, *Cheadle Coal Town*, 1981, p7) and from at least 1837 Richard Smith was farming 64 acres there. The house was not occupied in early 1881. WAAFs were billeted at the hall during the Second World War while working at Woodhead Hall. In 1986 the hall was described as having a 17th century core but had been rebuilt in the early 19th century with mid 19th century alterations. This grade II listed building, together with its considerable grounds, were bought by Mohammed and Parveen Siddique in 1990. They opened their restaurant at Thornbury Hall in 1994.

Watlands House, Wolstanton

A member of the Rogers family built this elegant house in 1816. It was the seat of Spencer Rogers, a banker. (1) Afterwards Lewis Adams, a pottery manufacturer, occupied the house until he died in 1850. (2) Edmund Thomas Wedgwood Wood, another pottery manufacturer, occupied Watlands House in 1871. He lived there with his wife and two adult children. Their household staff included a governess, lady's maid, cook, housemaid, kitchen maid, footman, page, groom and coachman. By 1881 Oliver Lodge, a merchant banker lived there. The house was in a neglected state by 1940 and was demolished in 1950.

Westwood Manor, Wetley Rocks

The old Westwood Hall, the home of Captain Thomas Powys, was a square, grey stone building, which was pulled down. Mr William Meakin, an earthenware manufacturer, rebuilt the present mansion in 1879. He changed the name of the house to Westwood Manor. (1) In 1881 William Meakin was living here with his wife and children and four servants. From at least 1896 until 1908 it was the home of James Meakin. Sir William Goodwin FGS, JP lived here in the first half of the 20th century. Later the house was owned by Enoch Haughton who gave it to Stoke-on-Trent Education Authority to be used as a special school for children. It is still used in this way and is known as the Cecily Haughton Special School.

References

Introduction
1. The Spirit of Leek, Volumes 1-3 and The Staffordshire Moorlands and Churnet Valley
2. Townsend, B., The Glory That Was Home, 1990, p.6

PART 1:

Alton Castle
1. Pevsner, The Buildings of England, Staffordshire, 1974, p.59
2. For more information on the Victorian rebuild of Alton Castle, see Fisher, M., Pugin-Land, 2002, pp.52-79

Alton Towers
1. Fisher, M., Alton Towers, A Gothic Wonderland, 1999
2. Plot, R., History of Staffordshire, 1686 (he visited the county in 1680)

Apedale Hall
1. Dyble, D., A History of Apedale and Chesterton, 2002, pp.48-49
2. Dyble, op. cit., pp.50/51
3. White's Directory of Staffordshire 1851
4. Dyble, op. cit., p.78
5. Trans. N. Staffs. Field Club, 1932-3, pp.122-124
6. Trans. N. Staffs. Field Club, 1934-35, p.79

Aqualate Hall
1. VCH, Staffordshire, Vol IV, 1958
2. Kelly's Post Office Directories

Ash Hall
1. The History of Ash Hall, researched by Allan Shelley and published in Six Town Magazine, Jan 1971
2. History of Ash Hall, op, cit.

Ashenhurst Hall
1. VCH, Staffordshire: Leek and The Moorlands, Vol VII, 1995, p.172
2. VCH Vol VII, p.172

Ball Haye Hall
1. VCH, Vol VII, 1995, p.235
2. Inder, P., and Aldis, M., John Sneyd's Diary, 1998
3. Bednall, The Leek Easter Book 1799 to 1806

Belmont Hall
1. White's Directory of Staffordshire, 1834
2. Brighton F., The Tale of Ipstones, 1937, p.44

Beresford Hall
1. VCH, op. cit., p.16
2. Sleigh, J., History of the Ancient Parish of Leek, 1883, reprinted 2005 by Landmark Publishing

Betley Hall
1. Speake R., Betley, A Village of Contrasts, 1980, p.87
2. ibid p.92
3. ibid, p.110

Biddulph Grange
1. Ferris, A. Biddulph Grange, 1985, p.11
2. Ferris, op. cit., p.11
3. Congleton Chronicle, 26th January 1896

Biddulph Old Hall
1. Beckett, J.H., Trans. N. Staffs. Field Club, Vol. LVII, 1922-23, 'Three Old Halls', pp.91-94).
2. Staffordshire Advertiser, 1st April 1854
3. Sale Catalogue at William Salt Library

Blythe House
1. Penn, C., Staffordshire and Shropshire, 1907, p.98

Calwich Abbey
1. Thomas, Nell, Mrs. Delany, An 18th Century Visitor to Derbyshire, Derbyshire Miscellany, 1970, Vol V, Pt IV, pp.224-28
2. Kelly's Directory of Staffordshire, 1908

Clayton Hall
1. Evening Sentinel, 26th October 1992
2. VCH, Vol VIII, p.78

Consall Hall
1. Podmore, W., Consall Hall Landscape Garden: The Hidden Valley Revealed, 2005. Published by Landmark Publishing
2. A.S. Bolton's diaries

Cotton Hall
1. Lead, P., Agents of Revolution, 1989, p.153
2. Lead, P., op cit., p.148
3. The Staffordshire Advertiser, 22nd August 1818
4. Roberts, F., A History of Sedgley Park and Cotton College, 1985, pp.117-19
5. Lead, P., op cit., pp.148 and 150
6. The Staffordshire Advertiser, May 12th, 1830

Crakemarsh Hall
1. Pevsner, N., op. cit., p 129
2. Bentley Smith, D., A Georgian Gent: The Story of Charles Roe and Co, 2005, p.484
3. Morris, C., ed., The Illustrated Journeys of Celia Fiennes 1685-1712, 1982, p.111
4. Anon, Ashbourne and the Valley of the Dove, 1839, pp.300-01, quoting Debretts' Baronetage
5. White's Directory of Staffordshire for each year

Dilhorne Hall
1. Pape, The Ancient Corporation of Cheadle, NSFC Transactions.1930, pp.11-12
2. Chester, H., Cheadle Coal Town, 1981, p.53
3. Kelly's Post Office Directory, 1860
4. Plant, R., The History of Cheadle, 1881

Etruria Hall
1. Bebbington, G., Staffordshire Life, 'The Story of Etruria Hall', October 1991

The Field
1. VCH, Vol VII, 1995, p.91

Ford Green Hall
1. Rowley, C., Ford Green Story, 1983, p.93
2. NSFCT,1955, p.76

Foxlowe
1. VCH, Vol VII, 1995, p.115

Greenhill House
1. Plant R., The History of Cheadle, 1881, p.159
2. Kelly's Post Office Directory, 1860
3. Plant R., The History of Cheadle, 1881. p.159

Greenway Bank
1. Evans, K., James Brindley, 1997, p.85
2. Wheelhouse, D., Biddulph, 1977
3. White, W, History, Gazetteer and Directory of Staffordshire, 1851
4. Kelly's Post Office Directory
5. Staffordshire Advertiser 5th August 1871
6. Ferris, A. Biddulph Grange, 1985, p.37

Hales Hall
1. Plant, R., History of Cheadle, 1881, p.148
2. Plant, op. cit., p.80
3. op cit., p.80
4. Johnson, F., Victorian Cheadle, 1991, p.74

The Hall House
1. VCH, Vol VII, p.88
2. Land tax returns, Staffs Record Office

Haregate Hall
1. VCH, Vol VII, 1995, p.238
2. VCH, op.cit., p.237
3. Miller, M., Olde Leeke, 1891, p.308
4. VCH, op.cit., p.237
5. Hine S. Around Meerbrook, 2004, p.97
VCH, op.cit., p.131

Harewood Hall
1. Chester, H., Cheadle Coal Town, 1981, p.124
2. Chester, H., op. cit., p.125

Highfield Hall
1. VCH, Vol VII, 1995, p.196

Horton Lodge
1. VCH, Vol VII, p.68
2. Jeuda, B., Rudyard Lake, the Bi-Centenenary, 1997, p.176

Huntley Hall
1. Johnson, F., Victorian Cheadle, 1991, p.71

Ilam Hall
1. Porter, L., & Robey, J., The Copper & Lead Mines around the Manifold Valley, North Staffordshire, 2000, p.188
2. Baylis, A., The Life & Works of James Trubshaw (1777-1853), 1978, p.14
3. Baylis, A., op.cit., p.14

Keele Hall
1. Harrison, C, NSJFS., Vol. 22, 1982-85, 'The Coming of the Sneyds, p.41
2. Goodway, K., NSJFS, op.cit., 'Landscapes and Gardens at Keele', pp.70-71
3. Goodway, op.cit., p.72
4. Goodway, op.cit., p.87
5. Phillips, T., NSJFS., Vol 22, 1982-85 'The Landlord and the Village of Keele, 1830-70 p.104

Knypersley Hall
1. Kennedy, J., Biddulph, 1980, p.46
2. Wheelhouse, D., Biddulph in Old Picture Postcards, 1977, p.17

Lightoaks
1. Department of the Environment, List of Buildings of Special or Historic Interest, 1986
2. Pigot's Directory, 1828
3. Johnson, F., Victorian Cheadle,1991, p.68; Wilson, P., Oakamoor Remembered, 2004, p.43
4. A.S. Bolton's Diary
5. Crosby, A., A History of Warrington, 2002, p.70

Longton Hall
1. Morris et al, Potteries Picture Postcards, vol 3, 1988
2. Warrilow, E., A Sociological History of Stoke-on-Trent, 1977, p.372
3. White's History, Gazetter and Directory of Staffordshire, 1851
4. VCH, Vol VIII, p.228

Loxley Hall
1. Kelly's Post Office Directories of Staffordshire

Maer Hall
1. Wedgwood, B and H., The Wedgwood Circle, 1980
2. Desmond and Moore, Darwin, 1992, p.12
3. White's History, Gazetter and Directory of Staffordshire, 1851
4. Adams, D.W., A Brief History of Maer Hall, 1975
5. Deardon, J., Tale of the Backbone, 1986

Moor Court
1. Wilson, P., Oakamoor Remembered, 2004, p.41

Oakamoor Lodge
1. Porter, L., Ecton Copper Mines under the Dukes of Devonshire, 1780-1790, 2004, pp.152-54, 156)
2. Wilson, P., Oakamoor Remembered, 2004, pp.15, 36, 152-53

Okeover Hall
1. Country Life, 1964, pp.172-176; 224-228; 568-572; 645-649
2. Plot, R., The Natural History of Staffordshire, 1686, p.227. Plot visited Staffordshire in 1660

Parker House
1. VCH, Vol VII, p.88
2. Cleverdon, F., The First Parker House, Chronicles, 1994, p.41
3. Cleverdon, F., op. cit., pp.42, 45
4. VCH, Vol VII, 1995, p.91
5. Sleigh, J., History of the Ancient Parish of Leek, 1883, p.30

Rolleston Hall
1. Cokin, T., Staffordshire Encyclopedia, 2000, privately printed

Shaw Hall
1. John Stubbs' will of 1703; Plant, R., History of Cheadle, 1881, p.224
2. White's History, Gazetter and Directories of Staffordshire, 1834 and 1851
3. Short, G., Around Cheadle, 1984, p.63

Swythamley Hall
1. VCH, Vol VII, 1995, p.189
2. White's Directory of Staffordshire, 1834
3. VCH, Vol VII, 1995, p.189

Throwley Hall
1. Cleverdon, F., 'Survey and Excavation in the Manifold Valley', Staffordshire Archaeological Studies, 1995, No. 5, p.20
2. Cleverdon, F., op. cit., p.20
3. Cleverdon, F., op. cit., p.27
4. Cleverdon, F., op. cit., pp.25-26
5. Hall, S.C., Baronial Halls [etc] of England, 1846

6. Niven, W., Illustrations of Old Staffordshire Houses, 1882, p.10
7. Private Coll., R. Hurt, with permission

Trentham Hall
1. Pevsner, N., The Buildings of England, Staffordshire, pp.283-85

Westwood Hall
1. Boylan, M., The Westwood Estate, 1996
2. VCH, Vol VII, 1995
3. Boylan, M., op. cit.
4. Boylan, M., op. cit.

Woodhead Hall
1. Plant, R., History of Cheadle, 1881, p.154
2. White's History, Gazetter and Directory of Staffordshire
3. Plant, R., op. cit., p.55
4. Johnson, F., Victorian Cheadle, 1991, p.74
5. Leek History Society scrapbooks
6. Johnson, F., op. cit., p.74
7. Short, G., Cheadle in old Picture Postcards, n.d., p.61

Wootton Hall
1. Howitt, W., Visits to Remarkable Places, 1856, 3rd edit, Vol 1, p.511
2. The Strangers Guide or Description of Alton Towers, Staffs., etc, 1872, p.24
3. Strangers Guide, op. cit., p.30

PART 2:

Dimsdale Old Hall
1. Ward, J., History of the Borough of Stoke-on-Trent, rpnt., 1969, p.117
2. NSFCT, 1941, p.125

The Mansion
1. Short G., Cheadle in Old Picture Postcards, 1985, p.45

Roaches House
1. VCH, Vol VII, p.194

Watlands House
1. Ward, J., History of the Borough of Stoke-on-Trent, 1843, p.159
2. Stuart et al, People of the Potteries, 1985, p.11

Westwood Manor
1. Penn, C., Staffordshire and Shropshire, 1907, p.26

References in the captions are as follows:
1. Pevsner – Pevsner, N., Buildings of England, Staffordshire, 1974
2. Plot – Plot, R., The Natural History of Staffordshire, 1686
3. Shaw – Shaw, S., History of Staffordshire, Vol 1 & 2, 1798 & 1801
4. Ward – Ward, J., History of the Borough of Stoke-on-Trent, 1843

INDEX

Index